T0381153

# ISRAEL'S
## INTREPID WARRIOR

*The Dauntless
Courage
of Samson*

AUTHOR OLIVER WRIGHT

To order additional copies of this book, contact:
Xlibris
844-714-8691
www.Xlibris.com
Orders@Xlibris.com

Scripture quotations marked KJV are from the Holy Bible,
King James Version (Authorized Version). First published in
1611. Quoted from the KJV Classic Reference Bible, Copy-
right © 1983 by The Zondervan Corporation.

ISBN: 978-1-6698-4860-8 (sc)
ISBN: 978-1-6698-4862-2 (hc)
ISBN: 978-1-6698-4861-5 (e)

Print information available on the last page

Rev. date: 09/27/2022

# DEDICATION

Israel's Intrepid Warrior: The Dauntless Courage of Samson is especially dedicated to my dear parents, the late Pastor John Oliver and Annie Ree Wright. Their dynamic teachings and careful spiritual modeling directed me to the source of my salvation and Christian experience.

Also, this inspirational narrative is dedicated to all of the devoted believers in Christ with whom I have had the privilege of being greatly influenced in the way of my Christian walk. I have been further enriched in the redemptive love and compassion of our Lord.

Equally, this informative and illuminating narrative is dedicated to all of the men and women who are seeking a closer walk with our Lord and Savior. My desire is that all of you would walk wonderfully in carrying out the will of our Lord.

Lastly, this inspiring narrative is especially dedicated to my lovely wife Celeta Clarke-Wright, and to all of our children, grandchildren, great grandchildren, and godchildren. It is my hope that the heart of each of you will be far more enriched in your trust in God.

And above all, to God be the Glory!

# Acknowledgments

I want to acknowledge the spiritual influence of the late Pastor John Oliver and Annie Ree Wright, my dear father and mother. These loving parents encouraged me to read the Bible regularly, and to grow in the knowledge of our Lord Jesus.

Additionally, I want to also acknowledge all of the sincere and dedicated believers in Christ who labored tirelessly to teach me the great truths of God pertaining to holiness and sanctification. A huge debt of gratitude goes to these dear saints who toiled tirelessly in the ministry to pave the way for my spiritual growth.

Above all, I want to especially thank my beautiful wife Celeta, who is working closely with me in the Lord. She worked graciously with me in proofreading this manuscript, and in providing valuable insight and advice when needed. Her loving and delightful support is appreciated.

Lastly, I want to give a special thanks to my son Jarvis for his artwork support. And for all of the exciting and original photos he has provided for this narrative. He has been faithful in supporting me in artwork for many of my writings.

# TABLE OF CONTENTS

# FOREWORD

One can easily look at the life of Samson and say, "what wasted potential". Like most people, you've probably at some point wondered, how did Samson made it to the Hall of Faith, as recorded in the book of Hebrews chapter 11.

After all, when you look at Samson's life you see a man who was strong before men but seemingly weak before women. A man who was made strong by the Holy Spirit, but given into the flesh. And through many subtle compromises, found himself captured by the enemy in what seemed like his ultimate defeat.

Yes, to some, Samson's calling appears to fall short. He had the potential to take God's people back to a place of worship and devotion. He had the potential to deliver Israel from the oppression of the Philistines.

However, through a unique and subtle way in being used of God, Samson did accomplish the purpose announced by the angel who visited his parents before his birth. And in his final act, Samson did fulfill the calling of God in delivering Israel from the Philistines.

Notwithstanding, what is inspiring and interesting to me is that when mentioned in the New Testament, the only thing said about Samson was that he was a man of faith. There was no mention of his failures. Not even a mention about his enormous strength.

In this inspiring book, Israel's Intrepid Warrior: The Dauntless Courage of Samson, Dr. Author O. Wright explores this historical figure to reveal some intriguing contemporary content. It's an exciting journey where Dr. Wright uses the historical information we have from Scripture so we can learn how to fight our battles today and accomplish our God-given purpose, so that God is glorified.

Dr. Wright helps us to see how Samson ultimately recognized his dependence on God. And when he died, God turned his failures and defeats into victory. His message to us is that God is calling us to a victorious life. No matter how badly we may have failed in the past, it is not too late for us to put our complete trust in God today. Only then we receive the enablement of the Holy Spirit to become victorious believers.

Without doubt, I highly recommend this book. It is informative, thought-provoking and inspiring. You will see a blend of God's sovereignty, His divine grace, Samson's humanity displayed in his human choices and his resolve to ultimately accomplish the Will of God. Certainly, you will gather valuable insights from Samson's journey that will help you in your own calling of God.

Marlon G. Samuels
Minister and Public Speaker

# PREFACE

Israel's Intrepid Warrior: The Dauntless Courage of Samson is a distinctively powerful, suspenseful, and compelling narrative on Samson, the strongman of Israel. This narrative is a very real, biblical account of Israel's deliverer filled with a host of refreshing words and scenes not duplicated in any other previous writings.

At this time in Israel's history, because of her disobedience, God had allowed this nation to be mightily chastised by the Philistines. In fact, He had allowed this Indigenous group to brutally oppressed and dominated His chosen people.

However, when these people of God turned from their sins and asked Him for help, His incomparable compassion responded quickly. And in their deliverance, He called Samson and equipped him with supernatural strength so that he could deliver them to single-handedly.

Therefore, this narrative dramatically shows, in graphic scenery, how this strongman single-handedly delivered Israel from the domination and oppression of the Philistines. And with this display of supernatural strength, Samson became the one and only real life superman.

Clearly, Samson is an interesting, historical character of Israel. He was specifically born to begin the deliverance of Israel from the Philistine's oppression. Miraculously given to Manoah his father and to his mother who had been unable to reproduce, this child was born a predetermined child.

Being a Nazirite from birth and raised in a traditional Jewish home, this child was taught all the ways of the Lord by his father and his mother. In fact, they introduced their child to all of the learnings for the Jewish male. But Samson had been born to be a warrior for Israel.

Therefore, as Samson matured, the Spirit of God began to move upon him to begin his particular calling. And he learned early that God would give him supernatural strength to deliver his people from their oppression.

Definitely, God wanted Samson to be an agitation to the Philistines so that he could engage them into battle with him. Therefore, his heart was stirred to travel to the land of the Philistines, for he was in great admiration of the Philistine women. But this was God's way of agitating the Philistines to begin the deliverance of Israel.

And, as time went on, Samson travelled to Timnath and met and fell in love with a Philistine maiden. His love was so strong that he married her. For he was being led of the Lord. In that, he was to agitate the Philistines with his association with the Philistine women. So that he could engage them in hand to hand combat to break the stranglehold of their domination.

In truth, after marriage, Samson presented a riddle to his thirty Philistine groomsmen. But the thirty groomsmen could not solve the riddle. And the agitation of the Philistines had begun to take shape. In fact, it began with the thirty groomsmen.

So, not being able to solve the riddle, these thirty groomsmen threatened Samson's wife to get the answer. And at the tearful begging of his bride, Samson gave her the answer, and she passed it on to the thirty groomsmen.

Samson became enraged and returned to his father's house. However, sometime later, he returned to Timnah to visit his wife, and learned that his wife had now been given in marriage to one of his former groomsmen. Of course, he became very angry against the Philistines. Then, he destroyed the crops of the Philistines.

However, when the Philistines learned that Samson had done this, they retaliated by burning to death his wife and her father. And in Samson's revenge, he slaughtered many of the Philistines. The battle for Israel's deliverance had begun. Then, he took refuge in a cave in the rock of Etam.

Of course, the lords of the Philistine wanted him dead, and sent an army of Philistines to the tribe of Judah to demand that the men of Judah deliver Samson to them. And when Samson had gotten consent that the men of Judah would not kill him themselves, he allowed them to tie him with two new ropes and bring him over to the Philistines.

But as soon as he reached the Philistines, he broke free of the ropes. And with the jawbone of a donkey, he slew another 1,000 Philistines. Definitely, God was using Samson to single-handedly defeat the Philistines. Ultimately, Samson, with his great strength, was to deliver Israel from the domination of the Philistines without having an army.

Later on, Samson returned to Gaza and met a young maiden. However, when the Gazites learned of his presence in Gaza, they saw a unique opportunity to kill him. So, they placed guards at the gates to kill him when he came to the gate early in the morning to leave the city.

But after spending about four hours with this maiden he decided to leave. And when he came to the gate at midnight, he found it securely locked. So, this strong man of God responded by pulling the gates off their hinges and carrying them up the top of a hill far away. In this escape, Samson returned home safely.

Finally, Samson travelled to the valley of Sorek and met a young maiden named Delilah. And he allowed her to influence him. Hence, his deep love for her became his downfall. For when the lords of the Philistine learned of their affair, they conspired with each other to offered her a sum of money to work together with them to find the secret of Samson's great strength.

She immediately agreed. And with her deceitful seduction, she enticed him persistently and eventually weakened him with her repeated requests to tell her the secret of his strength. Smitten with Delilah, he fell right into her deception. And, at last, he told her the secret of his great strength.

Then, the lords of the Philistines quickly took advantage of this weakened man. But, instead of killing him, they decided to humiliate him. They gouged out his eyes and put him in a Gaza prison to grind at the mill.

However, one day, the Philistine leaders presented a sacrifice in the temple of Dagon to their god for having delivered Samson into their hands. And while this temple was crowded with thousands of Philistines who had come to mock Samson, they called for Samson so that the people could watch him perform for them. And this was where God wanted him to be.

Therefore, as Samson was being led into the temple, he asked his guide to lead him to the two pillars of the temple to rest. Then, he turned to the Lord and prayed. And God heard his prayer and restored his strength. He had also asked to die with the Philistines.

Quickly, Samson took hold of the two pillars and pushed until the temple came crashing down killing him and everyone else in the temple. And through his death, he had killed more of his enemies than he had in all his life. Indeed, he had killed all of the lords of the Philistines.

However, when his brethren and all the house of his father heard of his death, they came and retrieved his body. Then, they buried him near the tomb of his father Manoah. Needless to say, Samson became known as the most famous judge in Israel for his great strength. And in obeying God's call, he delivered Israel from the oppression and domination of the Philistines.

# INTRODUCTION

Astonishingly, after having been delayed in the wilderness for forty years because of their disobedience, the children of Israel had finally reached the Jordan River, roughly less than fifty miles from where that had started. They were enroute to the land of Canaan; the land God had promised to Abraham and to his descendants slightly more than sixty miles away.

Indeed, after leaving the land of Egypt led by Moses forty years ago, these people of God were now prepared to enter into that land of promise. However, upon reaching the Jordan River, God would not allow Moses to continue to lead the children of Israel into this land of promise. For at the waters of Meribah Kadesh in the Desert of Zin, he became angry and failed to fully honor God.

Nevertheless, God enabled His servant Moses to see the whole panorama of this great land. And after having seen this glorious land, Moses died in the land of Moab and was buried by God in the valley of Moab. Then, God chose Joshua to lead the children of Israel into Canaan, this land of promise.

In truth, God told Joshua that His servant Moses was dead. And he was to lead the Children of Israel over Jordan into this land of promise. They were to drive out all of the inhabitants of the land and to conquer the land for themselves. And they were to remain faithful to His covenant given by Moses so that they would have great success in this land and find peace.

In Scripture, God spoke to Joshua and said, "Moses my servant is dead. Now therefore arise, go over this Jordan, thou, and all this people, unto the land which I do give to them. And every place that the sole of your foot shall tread upon, that have I given unto you" (Joshua 1:1-3).

God also said to Joshua, "Only be thou strong and very courageous, that thou mayest observe to do according to all the law, which Moses my servant commanded thee: turn not from it to the right hand or to the left, that thou mayest prosper withersoever thou goest. This book of the law shall not depart out of thy mouth; but thou shalt meditate therein day and night, that thou mayest observe to do according to all that is written therein: for then thou shalt make thy way prosperous, and then thou shalt have good success" (Joshua 1:7-8).

Courageously, Joshua obeyed the voice of God and carefully prepared the children of Israel to cross over the Jordan River. Then, he methodically led them into the land of Canaan. Indeed, with great obedience to God's command, Joshua and these descendants of Abraham successfully strategically marched into this land of promise.

And, in complete obedience to the command of God, they quickly began to conquer this land of Canaan. In fact, within seven years these Israelites systematically drove out several of those Indigenous groups in conquering this land promised to Abraham. Afterward, these people of God quietly settled down into what was called their Promised Land.

And for many years, these chosen people of Israel served God faithfully under the dynamic leadership of Joshua and the older patriarchs who lived after him. However, their faithfulness to God was not to be sustained. For not long after the deaths of Joshua and the older patriarchs after him, the children of Israel became disobedient to God and failed to remain faithful to His covenant.

In fact, these glorious people quickly turned away from God's laws and His ordinances. And they also ceased driving out all the Indigenous groups from this Promised Land as they had been commanded.

Therefore, God was not pleased with this sudden downward shift in Israel's faithfulness. And because of Israel's failure to remain faithful to His covenant, He used one or more of those Indigenous groups who was still in the land of Canaan to chastise them.

Hence, after having been in this Promised Land for more than four hundred years, these children of God were often in battle with one or more of the Indigenous groups of the land. And they had not found lasting peace.

Definitely, at this time, there were a few Indigenous groups still remaining in the land of Canaan; namely, the Moabite, Ammonites, Amalekites, Midianites, and the Philistines, who the Israelites often engaged in conflict.

However, when the Israelites acknowledge their transgressions, turn from their sins, and cry out to God for help, His incomparable compassion responds very quickly to their deliverance. Then, He sends them a deliverer who delivers them from their oppression and becomes their judge. Then, this judge leads them back to Him.

Sadly, during this time in Israel, having served under many judges, many of the Israelites became very disobedient and began to do those things which were right in their own eyes. And for their disobedience, God delivered them into the hand of the Philistines to chastise them. And this belligerent group brutally chastised and oppressed the people of Israel.

Undeniably, God allowed this Indigenous group, the mortal enemy of the children of Israel, to mightily oppressed His people. And these warlike people unquestionably became a thorn in Israel's side for forty years. For they constantly challenged Israel's army by invading their territory.

Historically, this Indigenous group called the Philistines were the ancient people who were believed to be the descendants of Noah's youngest son Ham. Earlier, this group of people had migrated from southern Europe to the east coast of the Aegean Sea.

And far a while, these ancient people were known as seamen for they established their villages and towns close to the Mediterranean Sea. However, as time went on, these ancient people settled farther inland in this land of Canaan.

Indisputably, these Indigenous Philistines resented the Israelites because they felt that they had taken away their land. And these ancient people were not pleased with the idea of the children of Israel gaining more territory in taking their land.

Therefore, these Indigenous Philistines felt that in order to prevent the Israelites from taking complete control of their land, they would have to conquer them and defeat them in battle. Hence, they developed into a combative group of people.

In addition to being militaristic against the Israelites, these Indigenous Philistines also appeared to be more advanced than the children of Israel. While the Israelites were using only bronze for weapons and tools, this Indigenous group had advanced and were very innovative in their use of iron. And iron was more superior to the bronze.

Moreover, the Philistines and the children of Israel also differ in their religious beliefs. The Israelites believed in the one God of heaven. But the Philistines worshipped many gods; i.e., Baal, considered to be a god of fertility, Astarte, considered to be the queen and goddess of war and sexual love, and Dagon, also considered to be a god of crop fertility. These ancient people were also very superstitious.

Unfortunately, it appeared at this time that these aggressive Philistines were mightily persecuting the children of Israel. In fact. these bellicose people had taken away all of the axes and weapons from Israel. And the few axes and weapons that were left had to be sharpened by the Philistines.

However, after being severely dominated and oppressed by these combative Philistines, the children of Israel returned unto the Lord, and cried unto Him for deliverance. Then, the Lord heard their prayer and promised to send them a deliverer.

Interestingly, God had promised to send the Israelites a deliverer who would begin their deliverance from these aggressive Philistines. And in His approach to bring deliverance to Israel, He had planned to use this deliverer in a most extraordinary way.

Certainly, God had intended to send a message to the lords of the Philistines. For this deliverer of Israel would be an intrepid warrior, and he would fight the whole army of the Philistines single-handedly. And, in so doing, he would become the one and only real life superman.

Miraculously, Israel's intrepid warrior would supernaturally defeat the Philistines. And with his great strength, the lords of the Philistines will know that there is no other God but the God of Israel. Hence, while Israel waited for God's help, the news of this deliverer was sent to a barren woman of Israel who had been unable to reproduce.

Samson's Father and Mother

# CHAPTER 01
# Deliverer's Birth is Revealed

Certainly, the Lord heard the cries of the children of Israel and relented in His punishing of them. Therefore, He came to their defense and sent to them a deliverer. In fact, He sent the news of this deliverer by one of His angels to a barren woman of Israel who had been unable to reproduce.

Actually, in those days, there was a certain man of Zorah whose name was Manoah. He was of the family of the Danites. And he was a faithful leader who was looked upon with profound respect. He was also one of those leaders who constantly prayed to God for deliverance from these belligerent Philistines.

This man Manoah had been married to a very beautiful wife for several years, but they had no children. For his wife was barren and unable to reproduce. Yet, he had great love for her, and she was the darling of his heart. In fact, they were very madly in love.

However, in those days his wife felt very much ashamed. For not being able to give birth in those days carried much shame. And she wanted to give her husband Manoah a son. Surely, she cried and prayed many nights for the Lord to bless her to become a mother. She pleaded with him to take away this curse from her soul.

Then, the Lord heard her prayers and sent her an answer. One day while she was working alone in the field, an angel of the Lord came near unto her. She was immediately startled when she saw the angel. For she didn't expect to be approached this closely by another man.

But the angel of the Lord quickly calmed her and said, "Don't be afraid! God had heard your prayer and you are going to be a mother. And you will give birth to a son. For God has heard the prayers of all Israel and He will send them a deliverer."

In Scripture, the angel said, "Behold now, thou art barren, and bearest not: but thou shalt conceive, and bear a son. Now therefore beware, I pray thee, and drink not wine nor strong drink, and eat not any unclean thing: For, lo, thou shalt conceive, and bear a son; and no razor shall come on his head: for the child shall be a Nazarite unto God from the womb: and he shall begin to deliver Israel out of the hand of the Philistines" (Judges 13:1-5).

Upon hearing this news, she became overwhelmed with joy. For she quickly realized that this man was no ordinary man. He was truly a man of God. Indeed, she was so happy that she didn't know what to do. For she had been told that her husband was going to be a father. Therefore, she ran to her husband to tell him the good news.

Happily, when she had found her husband Manoah, she shouted for joy. Then, she told him that she had met a man of God who had given her some good news. Her husband Manoah quickly looked on her in suspense. Then, she said, "He also said that I was going to have a baby, and you were going to be a father. And our son will be a warrior for Israel"

And while Manoah was trying to understand what she was saying to him, he heard her say that he was going to be a father. Then, he wanted to know what sort of man was this who brought her this good news.

But before he could ask her, she began to describe this man of God to him, "Darling this man of God who came to me resembled an angel of God. He made me very nervous for he appeared too powerful for me. I didn't ask who he was and he didn't tell me his name. For his presence was just too magnificent."

Truly, in Scripture, she said to her husband Manoah, "A man of God came unto me, and his countenance was like the countenance of an angel of God, very terrible: but I asked him not whence he was, neither told he me his name" (Judges 13:6).

Then, as Manoah listened closely, she continued, "This man of God told me that I was going to get pregnant and give birth to a son. He also told me not to drink wine or strong drink, neither eat any unclean thing. He told me also that this child I will give birth will be a Nazarite to God from the day he is born to the day of his death. And our son would deliver us from the oppression of the Philistines."

After hearing those words, Manoah looked toward his wife with heavy thoughts and with great excitement that he would be the father. But he wasn't sure how he was going to raise a warrior son who would defeat the Philistines. Therefore, he went to God and sought answers from Him.

# CHAPTER 02

# Manoah Sought for Confirmation

Certainly, Manoah had received some great news from his wife, that she was going to give him a son. And their son would be a warrior for Israel. But he needed more information about what exactly their warrior son would be born to do.

So, he went quickly to the Lord to clarify this extraordinary news his wife had brought to him about his son. After having been brutally dominated and oppressed by the Philistines for several years, and being told that he was going to have a warrior son who would begin the deliverance from them, he needed to have this exceptional news given to him confirmed.

Therefore, he sought the Lord very fervently. He prayed, "O my Lord, let the man of God which thou didst send come again unto us, and teach us what we shall do unto the child that shall be born" (Judges 13:8).

Immediately, God saw the sincerity of Manoah and listened to him while he spoke. He wanted to console him concerning his son, the future defender of Israel. Therefore, He sent his angel to his wife again as she sat alone in the field. And as soon as she saw him, she was very happy.

Therefore, she quickly asked this man of God to please wait until she gets her husband. The angel immediately consented to her. Then, she rushed to get her husband. And when she found him, she was so excited that she could hardly talk.

However, when she had sufficiently caught her breath, she managed to say, "My Dear, the man of God that came unto me the other day, he has come unto me again. Oh dear! He is here again! This man of God has come again. Come and meet him for yourself."

Happily, as soon as her husband Manoah saw the excitement in his wife's face and heard those thrilling words coming from her, his heart began to beat really fast. Then, he knew that God had answered his prayer and sent the man of God again. He quickly ran after his wife to meet this man of God.

When they both had reached the angel of God, they couldn't believe themselves. This man of God was waiting for them in brilliant color. Then, Manoah quickly asked, "Art you the man who spoke to my wife the other day?"

The angel quickly answered, "Yes, I was sent by God to tell her the good news!"

However, overflowing with excitement and thinking that he was just a holy man, Manoah said to the angel, "Now let your words happen. How shall we order the child, and how shall we do unto him?"

The angel quickly responded again, "Of all that I said unto the woman let her beware. She may not eat of anything that cometh of the vine, neither let her drink wine or strong drink, nor eat any unclean thing: all that I commanded her let her observe" (Judges 13:11-14).

And after the angel of the Lord had finished talking, Manoah looked unto the man of God and was startled. For he didn't know what to say. Then, he thought that he would ask him to stay for dinner. So, he said, "I pray thee, please don't leave us right away. We want you to have something to eat before you leave."

Immediately, the angel of the Lord said unto Manoah, "Yes, I will wait as you have asked me, but I will not eat of your meal. However, if you want to offer the meal as a burnt offering, you must offer it unto the Lord."

In truth, the Scripture said, "And the angel of the Lord said unto Manoah, Though thou detain me, I will not eat of thy bread: and if thou wilt offer a burnt offering, thou must offer it unto the Lord. For Manoah knew not that he was an angel of the Lord" (Judges 13:16).

Indeed, at this time, Manoah did not know that this holy man was an angel of the Lord. But he knew clearly what a burnt offering was. Therefore, he and his wife quickly prepared the lamb for the burnt offering.

# CHAPTER 03

# The Deliverer is Samson

Meanwhile, while the burnt offering was being prepared, Manoah began to engaged the angel of the Lord in conversation. Indeed, he tried to come more familiar with this man of God. Therefore, he asked him, "What is your name, that when your sayings come to pass we may do you honour?" He truly still thought that this man of God was just a holy man.

But the angel of the LORD said unto Manoah, "Why do you want to know my name, seeing it is secret?" After hearing this stately response, Manoah didn't bother asking the man of God anymore for his name. However, he continued preparing the burnt offering.

Therefore, after taking this man of God's advice, Manoah presented this burnt offering unto the Lord. In fact, he took the young lamb with the meat offering, and offered it upon a rock unto the LORD. Amazingly, while Manoah and his wife looked on, the angel did wonderously.

For as soon as the flame went up toward heaven from off the altar, the angel of the Lord ascended up to heaven in the flame. Manoah and his wife looked on in awe. But then, they were startled, for they didn't see the angel anymore. Instantaneously, they fell on their faces to the ground.

Definitely, Manoah and his wife knew then that this man of God was an angel of the Lord. Quickly, Manoah looked toward his wife and said, "We shall surely die, because we have seen God." Surely, he was now convinced that this man of God was more than a holy man. He was indeed an angel of the Lord.

However, his wife was much more calm, and she didn't show any fear. In fact, she said to her husband, "If the LORD were pleased to kill us, he would not have received a burnt offering and a meat offering at our hands, neither would he have shewed us all these things, nor would as at this time have told us such things as these" (Judges 13:23).

Certainly, after hearing those words, Manoah felt at ease. He then took his wife into his arms and comforted her, for both of them were very pleased with what they had seen and heard. They knew now that God had heard their prayers.

In fact, Manoah and his wife became very happy. Truly, they were one of the happiest married couple in their neighborhood. They were going to have a son, and they couldn't wait to be parents. They were also very happy that their son was going to be a warrior for Israel. They cleaved to each other with an enthusiastic love.

Indeed, Manoah's love and affection to his wife became stronger and stronger. She was the dearest and sweetest person in his heart. She was also very beautiful and had good understanding. Truly, he loved his wife as a beautiful gift from God.

Undoubtedly, he wanted his wife to know that she was loved. And with great affection, he quickly took her into his arms and kissed her tenderly. Then, with deep stirring emotions and sizzling pleasure, they became very passionate for their love could not be constrained. And she would not let him go.

Afterward, she discovered that the Lord had indeed heard her prayer for she had become impregnated. With blissful joy and satisfaction, she knew that she was indeed with child. And she couldn't wait to tell her neighbors.

Undeniably, she told her neighbors that the curse had been removed. For God had heard her prayers and she was going to be a mother! Truly, she also told them that she was going to have a son who would be a warrior for Israel. As she thought about what she was saying, she felt committed to observe everything the angel had instructed her.

Therefore, she remembered very carefully what the angel had forbidden her. She did not drink any wine or strong drink, for she didn't want to bring any harm to her son. For he would be born a warrior for the deliverance of the people of Israel.

Indeed, during those nine months of pregnancy, she and her husband Manoah both prayed together and asked God to help them to be good parents for the child. They were fully aware that He had sent to them and their people this blessed child.

Then, the day came for her to give birth to this miracle child. Some of her neighbors came to assist her with the delivery. But God had mercy on her, and the child was born very quickly. Indeed, the delivery of the child was quick and painless. And she gave birth to a son.

The neighbors were very astonished! In fact, they applauded her for the child was indeed a beautiful son. He was very alert and appeared very strong even at birth. Indeed, the grip of his hands were very firm and his eyes were piercing.

In fact, to them, he looked like a defending warrior. But the neighbors didn't know what to call the child. They wanted to name him after his father Manoah. But his mother spoke very quickly and said, "We will name our son Samson."

Instantly, they all agreed with the name his mother had chosen. For Samson seemed to fit the child perfectly. They began to question among themselves what would this warrior do for the Philistines were mightily oppressing them. Manoah spoke up and said, "The Lord will show us."

Then, after seeing this beautiful child, the neighbors returned to their home with joy in their hearts. They knew that the God of heaven had answered the prayers of Manoah and his lovely wife. They waited for the blessed warrior to grow up.

# Chapter 04

# *Samson Grows up in Israel*

Meanwhile, Manoah grew very attached to his little son Samson. He was very proud of his little man, as he would call him. And as soon as his son was weaned, he began to teach him how to obey and love the Lord.

Definitely, Manoah wanted his son to be pleasing and obedience to the Lord in everything he did. And he wanted his little man Samson to be prepared for the responsibility placed on him as an adult. Surely, he didn't want to fail him being his father.

Therefore, as the child grew, he prayed with him and read the Torah to him very regularly. He also took him to the synagogue every Sabbath. And when his son reached the age of accountability, he taught him how to pray and read the Torah.

Certainly, Manoah wanted Samson to be properly educated in the priestly demands of the synagogue. In fact, he wanted his son to be well versed in the rules and laws of the Jewish culture and traditions. For he had been given to them by God to restore Israel to her proper standing before Him as before. Hence, he thought someday his son Samson might be a Rabbi or a priest.

However, as his son grew up and spent time with the other children in the neighborhood, he seemed very happy around them. But his interests for freedom and personal expression were far more advanced than all of them. In fact, he wanted to know why he couldn't do and enjoy some of the things the Philistine's kids his age were enjoying. He was always asking questions.

His father Manoah tried to satisfy much of his son's curiosity, but he was completely unaware that God had placed these enlightenment observations in his son's heart. He had been born to be the deliverer of Israel from the domination of the Philistines.

Nevertheless, when his son Samson entered into his teenaged years, his father Manoah began to instruct him about the family responsibility of Jewish males more specifically. He began to teach him how to be a responsible Jewish male and father, and how to lead his home faithfully. Thus, he carefully instructed his son on what God had expected from the Jewish male.

Additionally, he also began to teach his son the plight of the Jewish people. He wanted his son Samson to be fully aware that they were under complete domination and oppression by the Philistines. He earnestly wanted to protect his little man Samson from the cruelty of the Philistines. For they often harassed the Jewish males for no reason at all.

Without doubt, Manoah wanted Samson to be careful when traveling alone to the predominant areas of the Philistines. For he had seen and heard many horror stories of Jewish males being treated very cruelly by being in the wrong place. But his son seemed puzzled and could not understand the fairness of it at all.

However, his father would say to him very seriously, "Son, it might not make sense right now, but you will understand it better when you get a little older." He wanted his son to know that there were many sufferings in the life of the Jewish people that were not fair, but they had no choice and had to live with it.

Of course, his son Samson was not in agreement with his people being treated cruelly and unfairly. He couldn't understand how a group of people could dominate and oppress another group of people and the oppressed doing nothing about it.

Nevertheless, Manoah wanted his son Samson to be aware of the unfair sufferings of his people from the lords of the Philistines. He told him that the Philistines had ruled and dominated them for many years. And it appeared that this domination could go on for many more years.

Most importantly, he wanted his son Samson to know that, despite the domination, he didn't have to be afraid. He wanted his son to be aware where he was at all times, and don't take anything for granted. He wanted his son to be careful when confronted by the leaders of the Philistines. For they don't take kindly the outspokenness of the young Jewish male.

Then, he began to teach his son the wisdom of selecting the proper mate for a wife. He wanted his son to be aware of the misleading sensuousness of good looks and tears. Indeed, he wanted him to know that good looks and tears can be deceptive.

Also, he wanted his son Samson to know that good looks and tears being alone can bring a good man to his grave. Of course, he wanted his son to choose the appropriate Jewish maiden who loved him. Indeed, he wanted him to genuinely love his wife.

Amazingly, as he taught his son Samson, he noticed that he was catching on very fast. In fact, he was grasping what he was being taught with ease. He seemed very eager to learn and mature. In fact, he was showing growth far beyond his age.

Truly, his son Samson had treasured all of his father's teachings in his heart. For he saw his father as a wise man and listened very carefully to what he had to say. In many ways, he wanted to be like his father. And his father admired his son Samson very much.

But his father didn't know that oftentimes God would manifest himself to his son Samson. In fact, He would give Samson little glimpses of his supernatural ability. And Samson didn't have the fear or insecurity that other young boys had. He could outrun, outwrestled, outswim the young males of his age. God was preparing him to single-handedly defeat the Philistines with his supernatural strength.

However, when his father observes his son working out in the field with the other males his age, he becomes amazed. In fact, his son Samson was very fascinating to watch. For he could do the work much faster than many of the older males. And he didn't seem to worry about the complexity or the difficulty of the job. To him, his son Samson was controlled by a greater power.

# Chapter 05

# *Samson Becomes a Young Adult*

As time went on, Samson grew up and reached eighteen years of age. At this age, he possessed the wisdom and knowledge of a much older person. Indeed, he had become a very promising young adult. And He had the confidence of a warrior.

And when his father Manoah saw how his son Samson had developed, he was very pleased. For he saw the growth and maturity in his son as that of a self-controlled and sensible young man. He was very proud that his son had truly taken the advantage of his learning years.

Unquestionably, his father felt very comfortable that he had taught his son Samson everything he needed to know to be a responsible and productive adult. He had also taught him how to keep himself safe from the dangers in this society. Hence, he felt very pleased in seeing how physically and mentally developed his son had grown.

In fact, his father Manoah was completely astounded, for Samson's interests and drive in life had developed far beyond the young men of his age. And he had become very independent in his actions and thinking. He appeared ready to go out and explore the world.

Indeed, Samson showed much more matured learning than the young men his age. He was very curious about the outside world and wanted to go out and explore it on his own. He felt too confined and cramped up in his little community of the Danites.

Truly, in spite of the many challenges and the difficulties of his childhood, Samson had indeed grown up to be a very responsible young man. He appeared very ready to go out and explore this adventurous and intricate world that was before him.

Definitely, his son Samson seemed very gifted about life, and was very clever about the society in which he lived. Truly, he was a talented leader and didn't seem to be too concerned about the domination of the Philistines. In fact, he didn't show any resentment toward the Philistines for the cruelty and hatred they had done to the Jewish male.

In fact, he seemed to have developed an unusual attraction toward the people of the Philistines. Truly, he interacted with them in a way that was unheard of among the Jewish people. He also didn't seem to be fully governed by the norms and mores of his own society.

Undeniably, Samson was also very fond of the young Philistine maidens. And he would toy with and make romantic advances toward them as he toyed with and made romantic advances with the maidens of his own people. For God was using this personal and social development to agitate the Philistines to come to battle with him.

Without doubt, God wanted to use Samson in a remarkable way. And He wanted Israel to know that Samson was their deliverer. For he will single-handedly overthrow the domination and oppression of the Philistines with his superhuman strength.

Certainly, Samson showed no fear or apprehension toward the enemy of his people. He appeared very comfortable when he was in the company of the Philistines. Actually, he saw the domination of the Philistines only as a nuisance instead of an oppression.

However, when Manoah his father observed how his son's interacted with the outside world, and particularly with the Philistines, he became a little concerned. In fact, he became frightened, for his son appeared to have overlooked the dangers of the past.

Indeed, his son Samson behaved as if the people of the Philistines were his friends. And around them, he had a heart full of confidence. Even the lords of the Philistines didn't give him any fear, for he knew his God was with him.

Yet, his father Manoah knew the frightful history of his people with the Philistines. And he had great concern for the safety of his son Samson. Certainly, he didn't want his son to let down his guard too soon and trust the Philistines too quickly.

Indeed, his father Manoah wanted his son Samson to get to know the people of the Philistines, for they had inflicted great harm to the people of Israel in the past. And they had dominated the people of Israel for more thirty years.

But his father Manoah failed to realize that the Lord had blessed his son Samson, and had started preparing him for his mission to begin the deliverance of Israel. And in time, when he is engaged in battle, He would bestow on him supernatural strength. And he will be the one and only real life superman.

Truly, the Lord had called his son Samson to be a warrior for the people of Israel. And one day his son Samson would, through his supernatural strength, single-handedly defeat the Philistines to rid them of their domination and oppression.

Meanwhile, after Samson had become fully an adult, the Spirit of the Lord began to move upon him at times. Indeed, while in the camp of Dan between Zorah and Eshtaol, he felt the dynamic movement of God in his life. Even the wild animals would avoid him. And when he is near them, they would quickly scatter for safety.

Truly, Samson became very conscious that God wanted to use him in a unique way. For he wasn't like the other young Jewish men whom he interacted with. Indeed, his interests seemed to be very different than theirs. And he could do things they could not do.

Even the young Jewish maidens didn't understand him. They thought he was too zealously attentive to detail. In fact, to them, he was too laboriously studious, acting more like a nerd or a geek. And he also appeared lacking in the popular social skills, and didn't seem to know how to approach them.

However, Samson was very emotionally, mentally, and physically mature. And he was eager to find love and start a family. Surely, he wanted to follow the Jewish's tradition and find a mate among the Jewish maidens. Yet, for some mysterious reason, his heart was more attracted to the Philistine's maidens.

# CHAPTER 06

# *Finds Romance in Timnath*

Excitedly, Samson decided to seek for romance among the maidens of the Philistines. Despite the Jewish's tradition on courtship and marriage, he was determined to find his kindred soulmate from among those people who were considered his enemies. Unbeknown to him, God had placed this desire in his heart.

So, one sunny afternoon, despite the danger involved, he decided to go down to this little Philistine town of Timnath. At this time, he was fully aware that he would be the warrior who would deliver Israel from the oppression and domination of the Philistines. But until now, he had not experienced any real difficulty from the Philistines.

However, he quietly traveled to the little Philistine town of Timnath. He had no idea that God was positioning him to begin his deliverance ministry. Yet, his desire was to find romance among the Philistine maidens in this small town.

Fortunately, from the corner of his eye, he observed a young Philistine maiden walking all alone who was genuinely beautiful. Indeed, this lovely maiden had those gorgeous eyes that sparkle, and those full lips that seem as sweet as honey. This maiden also had a charismatic physique that was perfectly toned, and she walked in rhythmic steps.

Instantly, his heart was completely taken by her looks and beauty. Certainly, to him, this daughter of the Philistines was dazzlingly beautiful from the crown of her head to the soles of her feet. And he knew that he would be very pleased knowing her. However, he wasn't as careful with the looks as his father had instructed him.

So, without waiting, he walked up to her to make his acquaintance. When he approached her, she looked toward him with a coy smile that was touchingly demure and sweet. And she showed him such courtly good taste and propriety. Indeed, she was very polite and calm.

Then, he asked her to allow him to say a few words to her. She bowed to him in courteous affirmation. And when he began to talk with her, she showed him great interest. In fact, her eyes twinkled to his every word. And because of her sweetness, his few words turned out to be many.

Truly, in his eyes, this maiden was delightfully lovely, and had such a soft voice that showed the tenderness of her soul. And as he observed her, he saw that she had a sweet personality that was as beautiful as an angel. In his heart, he felt that he could really love her.

Therefore, after he had talked with her for some time, he tried not to ruin what he had gained, for he had taken much of her time. So, he bowed and said, "Thank you for giving me your time and listening to me. I must let you go now for I have taken much of your time."

Quickly, she looked into his eyes and smiled. Then, she whispered softly to him, "Your tender words are so sincere, and I could hear more. For you are a man among men. I am so happy you want to take me into your heart!"

Not prepared to hear those words, Samson became lost for the right response. But as he was preparing to go away from her, he said unto her, "My dear, you are such a delight, and you are so lovely. My heart has found you to be true. Would you allow me to see you again?"

She quickly nodded to him in pleasing agreement, and said, "Oh dear, please come again, I will be very delighted to see you again! My heart feels joy and excitement that you have found pleasure in me. My dear friend, please don't take too long."

After hearing those words, Samson was very encouraged. Therefore, every few days he would come to see her. He also would bring to her a beautiful red rose. And she would joyfully greet him with a decorous embrace. They were quickly developing an attachment for each other.

And because of their attraction to each other, Samson and this Philistine maiden fell in love with each other very quickly. They had become a bundle of joy together. But he had not mentioned her to his father or his mother.

Nevertheless, his heart had become very fond of her. So much so, that in a very short time, he felt that he could not stay away from her. He wanted her to be part of his life, and he wanted to be part of her life. So, he decided to ask her for her hands in matrimony.

So, without waiting any longer, he knelt in front of her. Then, he said, "My love, I have known you for only a very short time, but my heart thinks of you only. You are my sweetest love. And I can't go on without asking you for your heart in marriage. I know a woman as beautiful as you has had many proposals. But this proposal from me is for real. Will you give me the pleasure of joining with me as my wife?"

Excitedly, before Samson could complete his proposal, this maiden immediately began to show immense joy and happiness. As she rejoiced, without giving his proposal much time to sink in, she said, "Yes! Yes, I will be very pleased to be joined to you as your wife! My heart feels so blessed you have chosen me to be a part of your life!"

And with those words, Samson was very excited! Even though his father and mother did not know this Philistine maiden whom he had selected as his bride, he could not wait to return home and share with them this great news of his proposal.

# CHAPTER 07

# Samson is Engaged to Philistine Maiden

Happily, with a heart filled with excitement and expectation, Samson rushed home to tell his father and mother the good news of his proposal. And when he found them, he was bubbling with joy. Quickly, they asked him why was he so excited.

Instantly, he responded, "I have found a woman in Timnath of the daughters of the Philistines of whom I am very fond. She fills my heart with extraordinary joy and satisfaction. Please get her for me to wife. I know I can love her."

Immediately, his father and his mother became very concerned. For they couldn't believe what they were hearing from their son. And after they had clearly understood what he had said to them, they were very puzzled.

Then, they said unto him very firmly, "Son, is there never a woman among the daughters of thy brethren, or among all my people, that thou goest to take a wife of the uncircumcised Philistines?" (Judges 14:3).

Of course, his father and mother knew that the lords of the Philistines resented the Jewish men marrying their daughters. And they didn't want their son to be hurt. So, they tried to discourage him for entering into such drastic risk to find a wife. Indeed, they didn't want to see their son treated unfairly.

Additionally, his father and his mother were very concerned for the safety and wellbeing of their son. For he appeared not cognizant of the norms and mores of their society by entering into such great danger without caring. And he was breaking all of the unwritten rules as well.

In fact, their son was boldly doing things in front of the lords of the Philistines what other Jewish men wouldn't dare to do in the dark. Now, he had asked to be married to a Philistine maiden. He was asking for serious trouble.

Unfortunately, his father and mother didn't know that their son's relationship with this Philistine maiden was of the LORD. He had sought an occasion against the Philistines. For at that time the Philistines dominated and oppressed Israel.

And with this marriage between a Philistine maiden and a Jewish male, agitation will develop. Then, the Lord could engage the Philistines into battle with their son Samson to begin the deliverance from their domination and oppression.

In truth, the Scripture said, "But his father and his mother knew not that it was of the LORD, that he sought an occasion against the Philistines: for at that time the Philistines had dominion over Israel" (Judges 14:4).

However, Samson was not deterred with his parents' hesitancy. He was in love with this Philistine maiden. Therefore, he responded to his father and mother, "Get her for me; for she pleaseth me well."

Of course, his father and mother did not argue with their son Samson. Despite some tears falling from his mother's eyes, they both tried to satisfy their son's request. So, they all started toward the Philistine town of Timnath.

As they walked in the direction of the home of their son's prospective bride, his father and mother had some great concerns. For their son was connecting with their enemies in a way that would make it very difficult for him to be a warrior against them. So, they were hoping that things turned out favorably for their son.

Meanwhile, on their way as they passed the vineyards of Timnath, Samson felt that something wasn't safe in the distance from them in the vineyards. Indeed, he sensed that a ferocious wild animal was trailing them. And for the moment, he felt that his parents' safety were in danger.

Therefore, he asked his father and mother to permit him to go and relieve himself in the vineyards of Timnath. However, he wanted to investigate the vineyards to see whether a wild animal was indeed trailing them.

And when Samson was out of their sight from his parents, he discovered that there was indeed a young lion following them. In fact, when he approached the lion, this young lion rose up and roared against him. Quickly, he stood still and began to defend himself.

Although he had nothing to defend himself against this ferocious beast, the Spirit of the Lord came mightily upon him. And he rent this young lion with his bare hands as he would have rent a young goat. And in this show of strength against this ferocious wild animal, God was preparing him for the fight with the overwhelming Philistines.

Nevertheless, when Samson returned to his parents, he didn't want them to be alarmed. So, he didn't tell them that he had confronted a young lion, or what he had done to the lion. In fact, he continued as if nothing had happened, so they would not be fearful or afraid.

And because of his calm behavior, they didn't suspect anything either. For neither his parents were aware of how God would use their son, or his great strength. They only knew that he would be the warrior who would save Israel for the domination of the Philistines.

Therefore, they continued their walk to the home of the Philistine maiden. However, when his father and mother reached her home, they were pleasantly pleased. For they saw how beautiful this Philistine maiden was.

Then, they began to talk with her and they found this Philistine maiden very pleasant as well. After talking with her and her parents, they saw how happy their son Samson was with her. For this young Philistine maiden pleased him very well.

And apart from how his father and mother felt about their son marrying a maiden from the uncircumcised Philistine, they consented to it. And Samson became engaged to this daughter of the Philistines. Afterward, he and his parents returned home to wait for the engagement period to pass.

Samson's Wife in Timnath

# CHAPTER 08

# *Philistine Maiden Becomes Samson's Wife*

Certainly, after Samson was officially engaged to his Philistine fiancée, he returned home to Zorah with his father and mother. He had planned to set his affairs in order with his parents so that he could move away from them to Timnath to be joined with his betrothed wife.

Indeed, despite his parents' disappointment in him, Samson was overjoyed that he had found his warmest love among the maidens of the Philistines. And he was looking forward to a long and happy future with this precious darling of his dream.

Therefore, after spending some time at his home in Zorah, he returned with his father and mother to the small town of Timnath to take his beloved bride and establish a home with her. He was very sure that she would bring to him the greatest happiness.

Indeed, he felt very pleased to be joining in matrimony with his sweetest love from the daughters of the Philistines. Although he was still relatively young, he was also beaming with delight for he would now be a married man.

Meanwhile, he and his father and mother began their walk to Timnath. The distance from his home to his beloved bride was only a few kilometers. But, as they walked, the roads were long and exhausting. Nevertheless, he was returning to Timnath to be united with his gorgeous bride, the Philistine maiden whom he had great fascination.

However, when Samson and his father and mother reached the vineyards of Timnath, he became very curious about had happened to the lion he had killed. Therefore, he asked his father and mother to wait a moment while he stopped to relieve himself.

Actually, Samson wanted to see what had happened to the body of the lion he had killed. Therefore, he quickly turned aside to look for this dead lion's carcass. He knew that it would not be discovered by anyone.

And to his surprise, when he saw in the carcass of the lion, there was a swarm of bees that had made a home in the lion's carcass. In fact, this swarm of bees had built a beehive and there was honey spilling out of the carcass as well.

Quickly, Samson, with his bare hands, took some of the honey and began to eat some of the honey right away. Then, he took a piece of the honeycomb with the honey to bring back to his parents. And when he came back to his father and mother, he gave them some of the honey.

Of course, Samson still behaved as if nothing was unusual with the honey. Certainly, he did not tell his parents that he had taken the honey out of the carcass of the lion. Being very zealous Jews, he knew his parents would be offended. And him being a Nazarite, they would have strongly objected.

Not surprisingly, his father and mother were very amazed that their son had found honey in this strange area. Nevertheless, without asking their son where he had found the honey, they began eating the honey with him. In fact, they quickly gobbled down the honey with delight.

Meantime, he and his father and mother continued their travel toward the town of Timnath. When they reached the place where his bride lived, they went unto the woman of whom he was to marry. Then, they satisfied the necessary bridal arrangement. And when the wedding ceremony began, his parents politely stepped aside.

Quickly, Samson was joined by thirty groomsmen from the city who were also of the Philistine whom Samson's bride had invited. It was a traditional ceremony, and at the beginning, these thirty groomsmen seemed very supportive. Then, Samson and this Philistine maiden were joined in marriage.

However, when Samson's parents saw the thirty groomsmen and the officials of the wedding that they were all of the Philistine, their concerns for their son increased. For they were very much aware that their son didn't know any of the people who were among the wedding participants. They thought that their son was much too trusting. His parents still didn't know that God had set all of this up to begin their deliverance.

However, after the wedding ceremony had been performed and Samson and his Philistine maiden were married, his parents quietly left and returned to their home. For they did not want to be part of the wedding feast celebration with the Philistines. And as they walked the distance back home, they had some baffling talk between themselves about their son.

Nevertheless, the wedding feast celebration began. Not knowing any of the wedding party, Samson still followed the custom of the young men. Certainly, he prepared a sumptuous feast for the wedding. And this feast celebration was to last for seven days.

Undoubtedly, when those thirty groomsmen of the town saw what Samson had planned for this feast celebration, they were very pleased also. In fact, all thirty of the groomsmen vigorously joined in the celebration.

But God had begun to set the stage for Samson to begin his agitation against the lords of the Philistines. Truly, He was now setting the stage for the Philistines to engage in battle with Samson to begin Israel's deliverance.

CHAPTER 09

# Groomsmen Threatened Wife With Revenge

Definitely, Samson was very pleased that the wedding feast celebration had begun. And he was also very pleased with his new wife. Indeed, he was very happy to begin the celebration of his beautiful love. However, since it was a spirited affair, he wanted to add a little amusing entertainment to the feast.

So, he said unto the groomsmen, "I will now put forth a riddle unto you: if ye can certainly declare it me within the seven days of the feast, and find it out, then I will give you thirty sheets and thirty change of garments: But if ye cannot declare it me, then shall ye give me thirty sheets and thirty change of garments." (Judges 14:12-13).

Unquestionably, by this gesture of this riddle from Samson, God was setting things in motion for the agitation. For he wanted to use this marital event in an unusual way to defeat the Philistines. And this riddle was the trigger to start the agitation to begin the mission for which Samson had been called to do before he was born.

Certainly, those thirty groomsmen were very happy to hear Samson's riddle. For they thought his riddle would be easy for them to solve. For the Philistine men didn't think very highly of the Jewish men's intellect.

But they had no idea how involved and difficult this riddle would be to know the meaning. Nevertheless, with a little show of arrogance, those groomsmen said unto Samson, "Put forth your riddle, that we may hear it."

And as those groomsmen looked toward him with a smug look, Samson spoke up very quickly and gave them the riddle. With great confidence, he said, "Out of the eater came forth meat, and out of the strong came forth sweetness."

However, after hearing the riddle, those thirty groomsmen became dumbfounded. Despite having negative feelings about the Jewish men's intellect, and that one of their maidens had gotten married to a Jewish man of low intellect, they were now very concerned that their intellect might come into question. And that they might have to give something to a man who was to be inferior to them as well.

Without question, those groomsmen were very puzzled for they had no idea what Samson's riddle was all about. And there was no way for them to know the meaning. Therefore, they were convinced that they could not explain the riddle. They became very embarrassed and startled by this man of a so-called low intellect

Undeniably, those groomsmen became very worried. Yet, they were determined not to go down into defeat by a man who they thought was intellectually inferior to them. However, three days had passed and they did not know the meaning of the riddle. They sincerely did not want to give any of their merchandise to this intellectually inferior Jewish man.

Without doubt, those thirty groomsmen needed to have an answer to the riddle so that they would not look intellectually awful and weak in front of this Jewish man Samson. Even though Samson was the groom, those groomsmen felt the need to compete with him.

So, when those thirty groomsmen could not find the meaning of the riddle, they weren't going to be outdone. Hence, they decided to get the answer through Samson's wife. They thought that since she was the daughter of their people, she would not turn against them. They were confident that she was a true Philistine.

Therefore, they hurried to Samson's wife to pressure her to seduce her husband to get the answer for them. They thought that, despite disappointing them and getting married to this intellectually inferior Jewish man, she would at least help them with the answer and not let them appear intellectually weak to him.

Of course, if she refused to help them, they felt that they had no choice but to commit violence against her. Therefore, those thirty groomsmen came up to Samson's wife with deep frustration. They were determined not to look intellectually foolish in from of Samson.

Quickly, they said to her, "Regardless of your marriage to this lower-class Jewish man, you are still a Philistine! Although we are superior to him, we don't know the answer to his riddle. We need you to help us! Get us the meaning of the riddle from your husband."

For a moment, she looked at those thirty groomsmen with puzzlement. But before she could answer them, they said unto her, "And if you don't, we would burn your house down with you and your parents in it. Have you called us to your wedding to take that we have? Is that what you had intended?"

In truth, the Scripture said, "And it came to pass on the seventh day, that they said unto Samson's wife, Entice thy husband, that he may declare unto us the riddle, lest we burn thee and thy father's house with fire: have ye called us to take that we have? is it not so?" (Judges 14:15).

<br />
CHAPTER 10

# Wife Betrays Samson to Avoid Revenge

Frighteningly, hearing those hurtful words, Samson's wife looked at those thirty groomsmen in total disbelief! Seeing and hearing the intense threat and anger from them over whom she had married, she became very terrified. For she was not aware that those whom she had chosen as her groomsmen had not approved of her marriage to her Jewish husband Samson.

But when she saw the intense rage in their eyes, she knew that she had to control their anger and prevent this serious violence from coming to her and her family. She knew that she had to quell this anger of the groomsmen and get them the answer. And she wanted them to love and accept her husband.

Therefore, she thought within herself, "I love my husband and I don't want to hurt him. I will explain to him that the life of my family was being threatened. For I want to protect my family from this brutal violence of the groomsmen. I must get the meaning of the riddle from my husband for the groomsmen."

Sadly, with Samson's wife attempting to satisfy those thirty groomsmen and prevent their violence, the stage had been set for the Philistine's agitation. Indeed, with Samson's wife involving herself to curb those thirty groomsmen's anger, God had also activated the tension from which the disturbance of the Philistines would begin.

Even though Samson's wife knew that the riddle was between her husband and the thirty groomsmen, she had to do something to prevent this violence from her family. But she didn't know how she was going to get her husband Samson to tell her the meaning of the riddle in time enough to save her family. However, she knew she couldn't ignore the groomsmen's rage.

Then, she thought that her husband was a very honest man and he loved her very strongly. And his great love for her was very obvious to all. But in order for him to tell her the answer to the riddle and to prevent this violence from her family, she had to make her husband Samson feel that his love wasn't showing strong enough to her.

Hence, she made the answer to the riddle an integral part of his love. For she wanted to restrain the anger of the Groomsmen. So, she began to weep before him and to accuse him of not loving her. In fact, she wept before him the whole seven days.

Actually, she said, "You say you love me but you only hate me. And you don't show me any love. We are to share everything. You have put forth a riddle unto the children of my people, and have not told it to me. I don't deserve this."

Meanwhile, Samson was very startled with this sudden change. So, he quickly responded unto her, "Darling, I have been nothing but truthful and kind to you. And I love you with all of my heart where there is no space or time. But I have not told this riddle even to my father nor my mother, and why should I tell this riddle to you? It is my secret for the celebration!"

<br />
<br />
<br />
<br />
20

In truth, the Scripture said, "And Samson's wife wept before him, and said, Thou dost but hate me, and lovest me not: thou hast put forth a riddle unto the children of my people, and hast not told it me. And he said unto her, Behold, I have not told it my father nor my mother, and shall I tell it thee?" (Judges 14:16).

Nevertheless, because of the threat, his wife wasn't going to give up with that response. The life and safety of her family was involved. Therefore, she continued her crying until the seventh day. In fact, on the seventh day, she looked extremely sad to him.

Then, her husband's heart was touched, and he couldn't stand to see her suffer any longer. Therefore, he told her the meaning the riddle. Yet, he didn't know that his wife was trying to avoid the revenge from the thirty groomsmen. However, as soon as his wife had gotten the answer to the riddle, she immediately stopped crying.

In fact, she behaved as if it was some sort of personal satisfaction. But within her, she had a greater reason for the riddle. Indeed, she quickly gave the meaning of the riddle to those thirty groomsmen who were waiting. Indeed, they were ready to execute their violence.

In truth, the Scripture said, "And she wept before him the seven days, while their feast lasted: and it came to pass on the seventh day, that he told her, because she lay sore upon him: and she told the riddle to the children of her people" (Judges 14:17).

Unfortunately, in attempting to appease those groomsmen and prevent their anger from destroying her family, she created a larger problem. In reality, she unintentionally betrayed her husband, and caused great damage to his trust in her.

# Chapter 11
# *Samson Leaves Because of Betrayal*

Certainly, those thirty groomsmen were very thrilled and satisfied when they had gotten the meaning to the riddle. And since the seven days were still in effect, they were happy that they didn't have to give Samson anything. Indeed, they were also very pleased that Samson's wife had proven to them that she was still a true Philistine.

Therefore, on the seventh day before the sun went down, those thirty groomsmen confidently rushed up to Samson. Then, they proudly said unto him, "We have the meaning of your riddle." And before Samson could respond, they said, "What is sweeter than honey? And what is stronger than a lion?"

Immediately, Samson looked toward those thirty groomsmen with great disappointment. Certainly, he knew his wife had given them the answer to the riddle. For no person could have produced the meaning of the riddle so precisely.

And he also felt that the groomsmen had engaged themselves in getting the riddle in some way. So, he responded to them and said, "If you had not pressured my wife, you would not have found out the meaning of my riddle." Of course, the Scripture said it unto them in a more straightforward way, "If ye had not plowed with my heifer, ye had not found out my riddle" (Judges 14:18).

Without doubt, Samson was hurt! For he could not believe that his wife would betray him in that way. Now, he felt she had cried before him so vigorously just to get the meaning of the riddle to give it her groomsmen. But he still didn't know that they had pressured his wife with death to her whole family.

Nevertheless, he was a man to his word. Therefore, he told those thirty groomsmen that he would bring their reward on the next day. However, instead of going back to Israel, he went down to Ashkelon, a Philistine town built on the shore of the Mediterranean Sea twelve miles north of Gaza. Actually, Ashkelon was one of the five chief cities of the Philistines.

In Ashkelon, Samson killed thirty men of the Philistines, and took their spoil. For the Spirit of the Lord had come mightily upon him. And he killed those thirty men with ease. Then, he brought the gifts and gave the change of garments to each of those thirty groomsmen of the city who had explained the riddle.

But Samson had become very enraged with his wife for revealing the secret of the riddle to the groomsmen. He couldn't understand why she would do something so painful and detrimental to their relationship. So, he felt that he couldn't trust her anymore. And he had no other choice but to leave her.

However, without discussing this issue with his wife, he quickly packed his belongings and began to walk to the door to leave her home. And when his wife realized that her husband of only one week was leaving her, her heart became terribly broken.

But she couldn't tell him that she was trying to avoid revenge from the groomsmen. And neither one of them knew that this agitation was of God. If she had known that her husband could protect her, she would have told him right away. And he would have easily protected her.

Definitely, she had no idea that her husband could have quickly stop their threatening. In fact, he would have effortlessly destroyed those thirty groomsmen as he did to the men in Ashkelon to get them their gifts..

And if Samson had known that his thirty groomsmen had turned against him, and were threatening his wife, he would have put a stop to it right away. Of course, he didn't know those groomsmen personally, but he trusted them as guests to his wedding.

Sadly, it was too late. His wife had done what she had to do. And Samson had made up his mind to return home as a result. However, knowing that there wasn't anything she could do, his wife rushed to her father.

Even though her father didn't know why his daughter's husband was leaving, and he didn't know that his life had been threatened, she came to him anyway to ask for his help. But he could only look, for he knew that Samson was his own man.

Then, as his wife watched her husband Samson walked through the door, she went to her room and fell upon her bed. Then, she shed sorrowful tears, she knew that he loved her, and now he was leaving. And she had not told to him why she had to do what she had done.

Indeed, Samson was kept in the dark about the threats of the groomsmen and he felt betrayed. Therefore, he quickly returned home to his father's house in Zorah. He felt he needed to take some time to cool down a bit.

In his heart, knowing that his wife had betrayed him to those thirty groomsmen within one week of marriage, he felt he couldn't stay any longer with her. Hence, the agitation of the Philistines had begun.

# CHAPTER 12

# *Samson Decided to Return to his Wife*

Certainly, with a disappointed and unhappy appearance, Samson returned home to his parents. And when they saw him coming, they were very surprised that he had come home so soon. They hoped he had not gotten any harassment so soon from the lords of the Philistines.

Truly, his parents were well aware that the Philistines resented their son's marriage to one of their daughters. For they did not like the Jewish males and didn't want their daughters producing any offspring from them.. Hence, they positioned themselves to hear what their son had to say.

However, when he entered into their home with an unhappy presence, he explained that in only one week his wife had become disloyal to him to those thirty groomsmen. She had given them the meaning to a riddle he had given them. I trusted her with the answer. but she gave it to them right after I had told her.

His parents looked toward him with some disappointment, for they were startled that he acted so fast. So, they quickly responded, "Son, your wife is a very lovely person. It is not like her to do such a thing. Do you know why she would deceive you in giving the answer to the riddle to those thirty groomsmen?"

Samson replied, "No, I don't know why she would give it to them when she knew how much it meant to me. I thought she loved me. But in doing this, she showed disloyal to me. And I can't trust her anymore. So, I thought it was best for me to leave her."

Even though his parents did not agree with him in his quick response, they replied, "Ok son, do what you think is best." They knew that their son felt betrayed by someone he loved and could not get over it right away.

Meanwhile, after hearing what his parents had asked him, Samson began to think. Then, he realized that he had not in fact discussed this issue his wife. So, after being at home away from his wife for some time, his anger waned a bit. And he began to reflect on what his parents had asked him.

Immediately, he began to regret not discussing this issues his wife. Then, he began to feel sorry for her. So, he decided that he would return to her home to comfort her. Truly, he wanted to see her again to rebuild his trust in her. For he still greatly loved her.

Therefore, after a few months, he told his parents that he was returning home to his wife to rejoin her. He was going back to the small town of Timnath and rekindle his love with his wife. Despite what she had done, he thought his marriage was worth preserving. For his wife was still very precious in his heart.

However, when his parents heard what their son had planned to do, they weren't too comfortable with the idea. For they thought that the lords of the Philistines didn't take too kindly to him marrying their daughter at first. And then, after one week, walking away from her. They were sure that these Philistine leaders weren't pleased with him at all.

Even though his parents didn't know that it was of the Lord that Samson would behave in this manner toward his wife, they urged him to be careful. They knew that their son's trust was still in the Lord, and he wanted to do that which was right.

But God wanted Samson to agitate the lords of the Philistines to the extent that he could engage in battle with them. For he had been born to be a warrior for Israel. And he was the warrior who would single-handedly deliver the Israelites from the domination and oppression of the Philistines.

Therefore, around the time of the wheat harvest Samson decided to return to the small town of Timnath to be with his wife. And after being away from his wife for some time, he decided to bring her a peace offering. Hence, he wanted to present to her a young goat as an olive branch of peace. So, he began the walk to Timnath.

Strangely, upon his arrival to his wife's home, he realized that there was much nervousness in the atmosphere of her home regarding his presence. And when he attempted to go into his wife's bed chamber to talk with her, her father would not allow him to go in.

In fact, her father said to him, "You had stayed away so long, And I truly thought that you had utterly hated her. Truly, I thought you didn't love her anymore. Therefore, I gave her to one of the men who was at the wedding."

Hearing this, Samson was appalled! He couldn't believe a decision on his marriage could be made so quickly. He felt that her father had not taken his daughter's marriage with him seriously enough. He also felt that her father had been influenced by the resentment of the Philistines.

Actually, Samson felt that he had been terribly treated. And this treatment of him appears inexcusable for him. But God was continually building the stage for him to engage in battle with the lords of the Philistines, so that he could deliver the Israelites from their domination.

However, when his wife's father realized that Samson wasn't pleased, he tried to appease him by asking him to take his younger daughter instead. In fact, her father said to him, "Is not her younger sister more pretty than she? Take her instead of your wife, I beg you!"

Indeed, the Scripture said, "And her father said, I verily thought that thou hadst utterly hated her; therefore I gave her to thy companion: is not her younger sister fairer than she? take her, I pray thee, instead of her." (Judges 15:2).

Definitely, Samson had become very furious again, and he began to think very deeply. He knew then that the Philistines resented him, and they weren't going to be fair with him living in their area with any of their maidens. He knew that racial bias and dishonesty toward him and the Jewish people would not allow him to enjoy living among them.

Hence, Samson responded to his wife's father, "Now shall I be more blameless than the Philistines? Well, I am going to teach them a lesson." He knew that this decision to give his wife to one of the groomsmen stemmed much farther than his wife's family. He knew now that his wife's father had been influenced by the hatred of the Philistines.

Unfortunately, despite the great love Samson had for his wife, he was never reunited with her. So, he thought he would make the Philistines suffer. And he felt that it was time for him to begin the deliverance of Israel.

# CHAPTER 13

# Samson's First Battle With the Philistines

Certainly, Samson wanted to punish the Philistines for meddling in his marriage. For he was very disappointed with his spousal situation! And since it was harvest time, he knew that there was no better punishment than to destroy their harvest. So, he decided to set their fields on fire.

And when he thought about what he wanted to do, the Spirit of the Lord came upon him. Then, he went and caught three hundred foxes, and took firebrands, and turned tail to tail, and put a firebrand in the midst between two tails. Then, he set the brands on fire, and let the foxes go into the standing corn of the Philistines.

Without doubt, Samson tried to destroy everything of the Philistines during the time of harvest. He wanted to stop them from interfering into his affairs. And he did burn up both the shocks, and also the standing corn, with the vineyards and olives. In fact, he destroyed their whole crop.

Certainly, God had set the stage to get the Philistines to engage in battle with Samson. For when they realized what had happened to their crop, they got very furious themselves and began to ask, "Who set our fields on fire?"

Of course, the Philistines of Timnath quickly spoke up and said, "Samson, the son in law of the Timnite, because he had taken his wife, and given her to his companion" (Judges 15:6). Despite the unfairness in what had happened to Samson, these Philistines of Timnath thought that they could destroy Samson very easily.

Strangely, the Philistines in Timnath became very angry! However, instead of getting revenge on Samson, they quickly gather around Samson's wife and her father's home. Then, they quickly set their home on fire. They also burnt his wife and her father with fire, for they thought they didn't deserve to live for being marriage to such a low-class Jewish man.

However, when Samson realized what the Philistines had done to his wife and her father, he became very angry with the Philistines. He knew that they had become very vicious in killing his wife and her father.

Therefore, he was determined not to let them get away with this violence. So, he quickly responded unto them. He said, "Though ye have done this, yet will I get revenge from all of you, and after I have killed many of you then I will be satisfied."

At this time, those Philistines were not afraid of Samson. They did not know that the Lord was with him and he had superhuman strength. So, those Philistines of Timnath gathered around the burned home of his wife and her father. In fact, there were hundreds of them who had gathered. They were like an incensed mob.

However, the Spirit of God moved mightily upon Samson. Therefore, he took a rod and single-handedly beat those Philistines hip and thigh. In fact, he thrashed these Philistines with a great slaughter. Certainly, there were astounded of the power of this one man.

Indeed, through the power of God, Samson had begun the deliverance of Israel from the Philistines' domination. For he killed many of the Philistines in Timnath and put many to flight. In fact, he had destroyed many of them as an army would do when it devastated whole towns.

Then, after he had gotten his revenge from the Philistines in Timnath for killing his wife, he left Timnath and went down to Judah and dwelt in the top of the rock Etam. There was a rock there with a cave near the town of Etam, where he made his home. This place was located in Judah in the low hill country.

Samson knew the lords of the Philistines would be looking for him. So, he went there to camp out. He also knew that God had helped him in given him supernatural strength to continue his revenge on the Philistines. Hence, he waited for the lords of the Philistines next move.

# CHAPTER 14
# *Philistines Tried to Capture Samson*

Meanwhile, the lords of the Philistines were incensed! After they had heard what Samson had done to the Philistines in Timnath, they thought he didn't deserve to live any longer. In fact, in their mind, they thought this Jewish man had gotten beside himself.

Unquestionably, these lords of the Philistines wanted to get rid of this menace right away. And they were determined not to tolerate this behavior any longer. They wanted to show this confused fellow who was his ruler. Therefore, they looked for him with the viciousness of a mob.

And when they had learned where he had gone, they rushed up to the land of the tribe of Judah and set up their capturing team with a few thousands of their bravest soldiers. Quickly, they positioned themselves in a small village called Lehi.

With this large posse of outraged men, these Philistines had prepared themselves to capture this trifling renegade with the greatest of ease. Then, they would pass swift judgment on him while in their possession.

However, when the men of Judah saw this large gathering of Philistines, they became concerned. And not knowing what was going on, they came quickly unto them and asked, "Why have you come up against us with so much force?"

The lords of the Philistines quickly responded, "To capture and arrest Samson have we entered into your land. Truly, we are going to do to him as he hath done to us." They continued. "This severely mentally disturbed man of Israel has killed many of our people in Timnath. And we are going to put a stop to him so this won't happen again."

After the men of Judah had observed the rage of these hostile Philistines who had gathered in their area, they were afraid. So, they had to do something to calm the fierceness of their hostility. Therefore, they quickly told them that they would get Samson and bring him to them. Then, these enraged Philistines gave the men of Judah two new cords to bind Samson.

With great honesty, three thousands men of Judah rushed to the top of the rock Etam to talk with Samson. As they rushed to get Samson, they talked among themselves about this great feat Samson had inflicted on the Philistines in Timnath.

Certainly, these men of Judah thought that in order for Samson to do this great feat to the Philistines in Timnath, God had to be using him in giving him this supernatural strength. For this great defeat to this large group of Philistines was far beyond any small group of well-trained men. They knew that he had been born to be a warrior for Israel.

However, when these men of Judah had reached Samson, they cautiously said to him, "Don't you know that the Philistines are rulers over us? What have you done to bring this kind of violence upon us? Are you out of your mind?"

Samson quickly answered, "The Philistines were angry with me for what I had done to their crops, then they killed my wife for no reason at all. They burned up my wife and her father and I wasn't there to protect her. These angry Philistines thought to hurt me. So, as they did unto me, so have I done unto them."

Then, the men of Judah said unto him, "The lords of the Philistines have gathered in our area to capture and arrest you for what you have done. They want to take you to their judgment hall. And we don't have any choice. Therefore, we have come down to fasten your hands and feet, so that we may deliver you into the custody of the Philistines. We all don't have to die for this."

When Samson saw how fearful the men of Judah were, he said unto them, "Be not afraid nor dismayed by reason of their great multitude. For the battle with the Philistines is not yours, it is the Lord! And you shall not need to fight in this battle. Prepare yourselves, stand you still, and see the salvation of the Lord. I will be used of Him. Now, swear unto me, that you will not fall upon me yourselves."

And they quickly said unto him, "No, we wouldn't dare do any harm to you. But we will fasten your hands and feet with these two new cords, and bring you safely unto the Philistines." Then, he submitted to them.

Quickly, the men of Judah fasten Samson's hands and feet with two new cords, and brought him down from the rock Etam to Lehi. Then, these men of Judah positioned this tightly bound Samson close to the area of the lords of the Philistines.

As soon as Samson was positioned so that the Philistines could see him, he bowed his head and prayed, "Our God, will you not judge them? For I have no might against this great company that has come up against me. Neither know I what to do. But my eyes are upon you."

Then, ferociously, as soon as those angry men of the Philistines saw that Samson was all tied up when he was brought unto them, they rose up in great fury. And with boiling hatred and wickedness, these angry men proceeded toward Samson to get him and bring him to justice.

Without doubt, they were very pleased with the men of Judah in helping them capture this outlaw. For they knew that having Samson's hands and legs fasten securely with those two new cords they had brought with them; they had gotten the advantage. They were sure he couldn't repeat what he had done to their people the day before. These angry men rushed toward him!

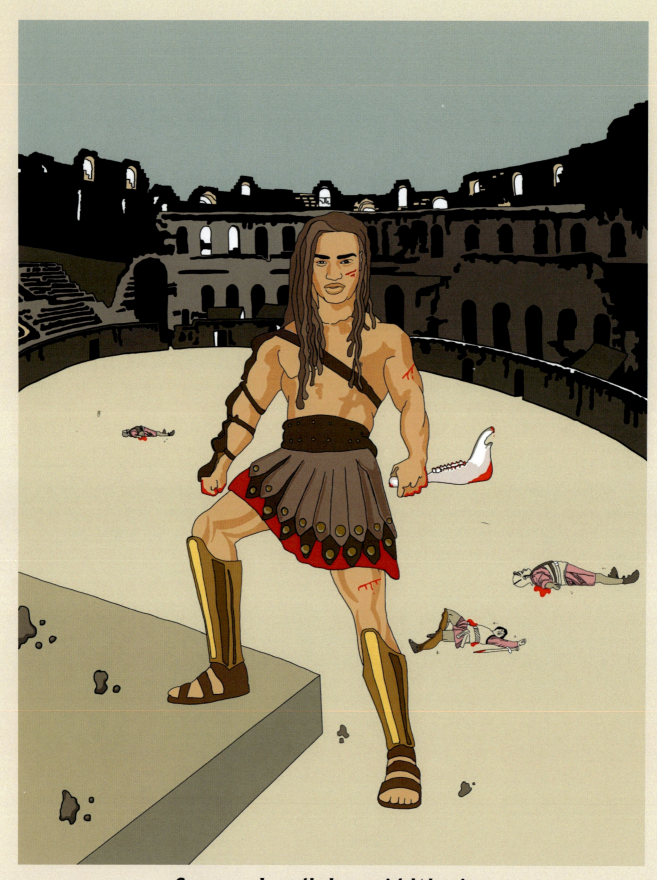

Samson, Israel's Intrepid Warrior

# CHAPTER 15
# Samson's Second Battle With the Philistines

Definitely, these lords of the Philistines were very pleased with the men of Judah in assisting them in capturing this dangerous man called Samson. They thought now his reign of terror had ended. Therefore, they quickly approached him with thousands of their soldiers.

However, when Samson saw that these angry lords of the Philistines and thousands of their soldiers rushing toward him, he trusted God for help. He knew these angry men were very determined to do him great bodily harm. But God had planned to use him miraculously in this battle.

Therefore, as soon as these angry men of the Philistines had reached him, they shouted against him. They tried to spread much fear and panic in him as humanly possible. But the Spirit of the Lord came mightily upon Samson, and the cords that were upon his arms became as cloth that was burnt with fire, and his bands loosed from off his hands. And he rose up instantly to his defense.

Even though this army had thousands of Philistines who were equipped with swords and spears, Samson didn't have anything to defend himself. But he quickly looked around for something he could use to fight this vicious mob.

Miraculously, he found the jawbone of a recently deceased donkey lying near him. It seemed that God had placed this jawbone there for him. Without waiting, he thought this fresh jawbone would be a good weapon to defend himself.

So, he picked up this jawbone and used it as a weapon to defend himself. He knew that God would give him the victory. For he was doing His will. And as these venomous lords of the Philistines charged toward him with all of their men, Samson began to defend himself.

In fact, with this fresh jawbone of the donkey, he whack these soldiers on their head and shoulder so profoundly that they were completely confused. It was like Samson had become an army of men himself.

Indeed, with this fresh jawbone, he was breaking and cracking their skulls as with a rod. And he only needed one whack to destroy them. For as soon as he hit the head of a soldier, he would fall down dead suddenly and not get up. For God was using him as His intended deliverer.

And, in so doing, he killed a thousand of those angry Philistine soldiers who fell dead lying on top of each other in piles. And when the other enraged soldiers saw what had happened to their comrades, they immediately changed their mind and took flight. Unquestionably, they ran like scared rabbits. And they quickly left the land of Judah in fear.

Then, after they had gone, Samson looked all around and saw nothing but the dead bodies of the Philistines he had killed. He said, "With the jawbone of a donkey, piles upon piles, with the jaw of a donkey have I slain a thousand of those troopers." And as soon as he had finished saying this, he threw the jawbone back to the ground. Then, he called that place Ramathlehi.

Afterward, because of the intense battle and the heat, he became very thirsty, that he thought he was going to die. Then, he called on the Lord, and said, "Thou hast given this great deliverance into the hand of thy servant: and now shall I die for thirst, and fall into the hand of these uncircumcised Philistines?" (Judges 15:18).

But God quickly bore an hollow place in the jawbone, and water came pouring out. And when he had drunk, his spirit came again. And he revived. Wherefore, he called the name of that spot Enhakkore, which is in Lehi unto this day.

Meanwhile, from a distance, those timid and fearful men of Judah who had brought Samson to the lords of the Philistines carefully observe what would happen to him. And they saw the quick reactions of those angry Philistines.

For as soon as they had positioned Samson close to them and had walked away, those infuriated soldiers of the Philistines rushed aggressively toward him. In fact, they came toward him with the malice and bitterness of wild carnivorous animals who had overwhelmed a captured prey.

But when those men of Judah saw how quickly Samson rose up and began to destroy those soldiers with ease, they were completely astounded. Truly, Samson sprung up and destroyed those enraged Philistine soldiers as if he were some sort of superman. Indeed, with machine like movement, he indeed whack them down to the ground.

However, as those men of Judah continually to observe, they saw how fast those incensed Philistine soldiers retreated from Samson. In fact, those angry men of the Philistines withdrew hurriedly from him to save their own lives and wellbeing.

After seeing this, those men of Judah were thoroughly convinced that there was something supernatural about their Hebrew brother called Samson. For he showed the strength of a hundred men. He single-handedly obliterated a whole multitude of those aggressive men of the Philistines. He proved to be the warrior that he was acclaimed to be. They wondered what more could this man do for them.

# CHAPTER 16

## *The New Judge of Israel*

Certainly, this battle scene between Samson and the soldiers of the Philistines was captivating! And as these three thousands men of Judah observed this heated battle, they were completely in awe. For Samson had taken the jawbone of a donkey and killed an army of the Philistine soldiers who had come after him with swords and spears. In fact, their dead bodies were scattered all over the ground, stacked on top of each other.

Astonishingly, Samson appeared to be under some kind of trance as he defended himself against the Philistine soldiers. And when these men of Judah watched as the battle was raging, they saw Samson as a one-man wrecking crew. For he didn't show any physical or mental exhaustion during the battle.

And after the battle was over, these three thousands men of Judah rushed up to Samson and quickly noticed that he had begun to drink water from the same weapon he had used to kill the Philistine soldiers. To them, it was an indescribable phenomenon.

However, they quickly asked him how did he defeat this large number of Philistines. Instantly, he stated that it was a miraculous victory for him from the Lord. The Spirit of God had helped him killed those Philistine soldiers. And he was carrying out the deliverance he had been called to do. And this victory was to confirm the prayers of Israel.

Then, those men of Judah knew everything that had been said about Samson was true. He was indeed sent of God to be the warrior who would deliver Israel. For in this battle, he had killed a thousand soldiers, and had sent a thousand more soldiers into flight.

And when all of those men of Judah realized that Samson had single-handedly defeated an army of the Philistines, they knew then they had found their leader. Therefore, they decided to ask him to be their judge.

Definitely, those three thousands men of Judah got together and called for all of the leaders of Israel. Then, they described to them what they had seen in this great battle between Samson and the soldiers of lords of the Philistines in this small village called Lehi.

Quickly, they asked, "After single-handedly defeating an army of the Philistines, what more can this man do for us than be our Judge?" All Israel agreed and Samson quietly became their judge. But his judgeship was very unconventional, for he didn't have an army as the other judges had.

Meanwhile, when those frightened soldiers of the Philistines returned to their leaders, they reported that this man called Samson had caused great havoc among their comrades. In fact, they declared that he had killed hundreds of their people in Timnath, and now he had killed a thousand of their soldiers who had come to apprehend him. They proclaimed that with his superhuman strength, he couldn't be defeated.

Therefore, they quickly acknowledged among themselves that they had to make some immediate changes in their attitude toward the Hebrew people. They had to be much kinder in how they now approached them. For if there was one of those Jewish men with this superhuman strength, who can say there aren't any more.

Then, the lords of the Philistines quickly affirmed that this Hebrew man Samson was a phenomenally strong man. And they had to find the source of this man's strength. They thought that possibly he had gotten help from his God.

In fact, the lords of the Philistines knew that the Hebrew God had helped his people before. Therefore, they cautioned their people on how to be more friendly and peaceful toward the Jewish people until they could find the source of Samson's strength. They readily admitted that if we continue to dominate them, we will all be dead.

So, the lords of the Philistines and all of the Philistine leaders quietly ended their domination of the Jewish people. They knew that as long as Samson was alive, they would not be able to rule the Jewish people in the same manner as before. And there was an instant visible change in their attitude toward the Hebrew people. Yet, they still sought for the source of Samson's strength.

Definitely, Samson did teach the lords of the Philistines a lesson. For after this battle between Samson and the Philistines in this small village called Lehi, the people of Israel noticed a sudden change in their attitude toward them. Even though the lords of the Philistines watched the Israelites closely, they wouldn't dare harass them anymore.

Then, Samson became the judge of all Israel, and he judged Israel for twenty years. Although he didn't have the servants other judges had. He was more of a great, big brother symbol. For his charismatic presence preserved the peace.

Even though he judged Israel in a way that was very unconventional, he was respected because of his superhuman strength to defend them. And the lords of the Philistines kept their distance because of his great strength.

# CHAPTER 17

## *Samson is Now a Wanted Man*

Cautiously, the lords of the Philistines kept a constant surveillance on Samson. Even though they had abandoned their domination of the people of Israel, they still feared this strong man who had destroyed many of their people. Certainly, he had become a wanted man to them and they were determined to kill him.

Undoubtedly, the lords of the Philistines were acutely aware that Samson had single-handedly killed many of their people. And they were consciously aware that he confronted thousands of their soldier with nothing but his bare hands and destroys many of them without even getting a scratch on him.

But now this killer of their people had become the judge over Israel. And being the judge, the lords of the Philistines knew very well that Israel's judge was heavily protected by his people. So, they could not easily get close to him.

Definitely, the lords of the Philistines knew that the people of Israel had set up a strong defense to protect their judge. And they were well aware that they had established a careful watch for the safety and wellbeing of this leader.

Unquestionably, the lords of the Philistines knew that Samson had brought great deliverance to the people of Israel. And through his great strength alone, he had rid them of their domination. Therefore, his people would be determined to protect their honored leader from any covert attack from them.

Nevertheless, despite being the judge of Israel, Samson was still a marked man in the eyes of the lords of the Philistines. For they were terribly afraid of him. And they were determined to capture this enemy of theirs, and get revenge from this killer of their people.

However, they knew that their efforts to kill him would be futile if they tried to apprehend him in his territory. So, the lords of the Philistines knew that the only way to capture this strong man of Israel was to seize him when he was frequenting their area.

Undoubtedly, the lords of the Philistines had set up a sophisticated network of spying to capture and destroy this killer of their people. And they began to diligently watch for him traveling in their area.

In fact, a bounty was placed on Samson's head to anyone who knew his whereabout in their area. Without doubt, all of the provincial leaders were on the constant lookout for this most wanted man. All over the land of the Philistines there was a continuous watch for him.

Undeniably, the lords of the Philistines felt they had to find a way to stop this man Samson. For his great feat of killing thousands of them had so impressed the people of Israel that they were now thinking about dominating them. Clearly, the lords of the Philistines desperately wanted to know what was the source of this man's great strength.

Indisputably, by this time, the lords of the Philistines had carefully studied the daily routine of Samson. They knew a lot about the habits and behaviors of this strong man of Israel. And having spies trailing him almost every hour of the day, they kept a clandestine watch on every place he visited. Surely, they closely monitored many of the places he traveled outside of Israel.

Certainly, they knew Samson's likes and dislikes. And they were indeed knowledgeable that, despite him being a judge of Israel, he was often seen in the company of many of the young Philistine's maidens in his land. They knew that the young Philistine maidens were his favorites.

Definitely, the lords of the Philistines were aware that Samson is known to frequent with the young Philistine maidens in every opportunity he could get in his area. And they were also told that he secretly ventured into their area to meet with the young Philistine maidens. So, they waited to capture him in one of his daring ventures to their land.

However, Samson was well aware of the bounty placed on him. And being a wanted man by the lords of the Philistines, he was also very aware of their spying, and their desire to do him great bodily harm. But even with the spies and bounty, he would not stop his traveling to their area.

Therefore, he used great caution when traveling to the Philistine's areas. In fact, he only traveled to their areas in the darkness of the night. Yet, he was not afraid of the threats of the Philistines for he knew that God was protecting him.

Hence, since Samson occasionally traveled to the Philistines' area covertly, the lords of the Philistines had thoroughly informed the officers in all of their cities to carefully watch the gates to their cities. For this strong man of Israel was as cunning as a cat of the night.

# Chapter 18
## Risky Travel to Gaza

Meanwhile, one night, Samson had become very restless and decided to go to one of the Philistine's area for the evening to spend some social time with the ladies. However, he was well aware that the lords of the Philistines were closely watching him. So, he knew that he would have to travel in disguise to any of the Philistine's towns.

Therefore, under the cover of darkness, he left the safety of the Jewish people and traveled to the cosmopolitan town of Gaza in the Philistine's area. He reached this multiethnic town when there were only a few stars in the sky and the moon gave a blurry light. And there was no obvious suspicion that he had arrived in their town.

The moon had cast its blurry light over the town but the weather was clear and very favorable. Therefore, Samson moved closer to the people to join in with them. And after surveying the area and not seeing any possibility of threat, he went straight to one of the hot spots that was very socially active.

Indeed, as he carefully strolled through this lively multiethnic town, he felt unusually optimistic about this night. For he found this town very much alive. And he had great hopes to enjoy some fun time with the beautiful young ladies on this night's visit. In fact, he had prepared to spend the night and return home early the next day.

Undoubtedly, this multicultural and sophisticated town was very socially active this night. For there were loving couples going back and forth. And this town seemed to live up to its reputation by some as a lover's paradise.

And when he reached his social hot spot, he felt an unusual presence of fortune. For as he looked across the street, he saw a sparkling angel eye young maiden whom he recognized to be a Philistine walking all alone very slowly near this social hot spot.

Indeed, she appeared to be just the type of woman he had come here to meet. So, he decided to move closer to get more acquainted with her. Therefore, he carefully walked closer to the area where this young lady was walking. He wanted to be sure that there wasn't any potential threat he had to be concerned about.

And when he had gotten closer to this beautiful your maiden, he noticed that she was very attractive. Indeed, she had a beautiful physique and was very curvaceously appealing. In fact, she was dressed very irresistibly and captivating. And her chiseled face glowed with a dazzling affectionate smile.

Then, he decided to approach this beautiful young maiden. And when he had gotten close to her, she quickly stopped and looked toward him and gave him a gorgeous smile. Indeed, she was as charming as an angel. Immediately, he was drawn to her and wanted to talk with her.

Even though she appeared to be expecting someone, his heart reached out to her. And he wanted to meet her. Therefore, he walked up to her and stood right in front of her. But before he could say anything to her, she smiled glowingly toward him.

Then, she opened her mouth and greeted him very courteously, "My dear gentleman, how are you tonight? Are you enjoying yourself?"

And when she spoke to him, a joyous presence of her sweet affection was showered all over him. Indeed, the way this maiden spoke to him was so soft and unexpected. In fact, he was mesmerized with her rich gracefulness and elegance.

However, most of all, Samson was tremendously captivated by her intriguing, kissable lips. Actually, there was sizzling romance emanating from the soft movement of her lips. And they appeared kissably soft.

Moreover, the sultry and tantalizing sweetness in her mannerism compelled him to return the greeting to her very approvingly. Therefore, he spoke to her in his most masculine voice, "My dear love, you are so delightfully beautiful. Are you alone tonight?"

Quickly, as soon as Samson had opened his mouth to talk with her, she became a little surprised for she had recognized him. Then, she asked, "Aren't you Samson, the strong man from Israel who our leaders are looking for?"

Of course, as soon as she realized what she had asked, she paused momentarily to catch her breath. For she knew the risk involved in his coming to her town of Gaza. Then, she whispered very low to him, "Are you really Samson?"

Samson replied, "Yes, I am he."

She then responded, "Oh, you are so brave! You took a lot of risk to come to this Philistine's town! Darling, please be careful around here, our people fear you, but you are safe with me."

Samson quickly replied, "Thanks, you are indeed my heart. I will be safe." Then, with a sweet and interesting smile. She whispered, "Yes, my dear, I am alone!"

# CHAPTER 19

# A Night of Dalliance

Unquestionably, this Philistine maiden became very thrilled to be talking with Israel's strong man. With great excitement, she looked toward him with a warm and affectionate smile. Then, she said, "I had wanted to meet you, and you are here. Why are you here? Did you come to see me?"

Instantly, Samson was very delighted to hear those words. So, he replied, "Yes, my love! Indeed, you are the first person I have met tonight. And I have found the one who would make my heart feels joy!"

Then, she quickly looked into his eyes and put her hand on his shoulder. And with a deep amount of joyous satisfaction, she said, "Well, here I am! My dear, take me to the delight of your pleasure!"

For she knew immediately why this strong man Samson had risked leaving his home to come to her town of Gaza. Indeed, he had come to enjoy some time with the beautiful ladies. And she also felt that he being the judge of Israel, he could reward her with great gifts.

Therefore, they began to talk with each other for more affably. And as they talked, she pleasurably enjoyed all of his serenading of her. Indeed, she was very pleasantly pleased with the romantic beauty coming from his words.

Despite being a judge of Israel, she discovered that this powerful man of Israel was very soft and caring. In fact, to her, he was like any other ordinary man. He indeed had great love and respect for the beautiful ladies. And he appeared to be a man among men.

Also, this maiden had observed, during their conversation, that this strong man of Israel had become deeply attracted to her. For his eyes would not leave her. In fact, he constantly observed her every move with great admiration. And his hands handled her as delicately as he would his favorite flower.

However, most of all, she loved this strong man Samson for his noticeable gallantry. And she was extremely impressed with his superior ability to defend himself against great odds. To her, he was the most incredible man she would ever meet.

Now, having met him, she did not want him to leave her. Indeed, she truly admired this strong man of Israel and definitely wanted him to spend some time with her. She wanted to know the truth about this defender of Israel.

But then she remembered that she wasn't the only lady in this area. Indeed, there were many other beautiful young ladies who were also very busy in the area. So, in order to keep this strong man for herself, she tried to spice up their conversation. Since she was the first lady whom he had met this night in Gaza, she didn't want him to slip away from her.

Indeed, meeting Samson had brought great joy and pleasure to her evening. Therefore, she decided to raise the romantic passion in their conversation. She had hope that he, being a man, would be pleased to be with her only. Hence, she added a little amorousness to their conversation. She had also promised him there was some passionate pleasure waiting for him at her home.

However, in so doing, she inadvertently revealed to him why she was all alone on the street. And he discovered that she was not a damsel in distress. But she was in fact a lady of the evening. Indeed, she was a harlot, a woman of the street.

But Samson was now strongly attracted to her. So, he would not leave her. And their conversation slowly drifted to spending time with her as well. Ultimately, the conversation led to the discussion of exchange.

Then, after an agreement had been reached between the two of them for spending time with her, she warmly invited him to her home to enjoy some of her time in private. They quickly began the casual walk to her home.

In truth, the Scripture clearly stated, "Then went Samson to Gaza, and saw there an harlot, and went in unto her" (Judges 16:1).

However, while Samson and this Philistine maiden talked on the way to her home, Samson became very alert. For he had noticed that there was a suspicious man following him. Indeed, he thought he had been seen by one of the spies of the lords of the Philistines.

And from a distance, he got a good look at this suspicious man whom he had suspected to be a spy. Certainly, this suspicious man did appear to be a spy for he carefully watched him. Even though he was dressed casually, he appeared to be working undercover for the officers of the Gazites.

Nevertheless, Samson was not terribly concerned, for he was prepared to do whatever was required to protect himself from harm. And he knew that his God would protect him, for that is the reason he had been born.

# CHAPTER 20
# *Observed by the Gazites*

Certainly, while Samson engaged in lively conversation with this beautiful young maiden on the way to her home, from the corner of his eye, he had observed this suspicious man who appeared to be a spy watching them very closely.

But he pretended not to be startled by this suspicious man so he would not frighten this young maiden who was completely unaware of the threats that surrounded him. Indeed, she appeared to be more interested in making a living for herself. And she appeared completely innocence to the potential threats against his life.

However, Samson did inquire into her cleverly to see whether she had any connection with those who wanted to cause him harm. Thankfully, after talking inquiringly with the maiden, he discovered that she was indeed all alone. And there was no one from the lords of the Philistines connected with her to attack him. She wasn't even aware that there were spies in this area on the lookout for him.

Meantime, in an instant, this suspicious man, who appeared to be a spy, realizing that this man he had observed was indeed Samson, quickly left from his watching of him. Apparently, this suspicious man went hurriedly to the officer of the Gazites and informed them that Samson was in their town.

This suspicious man didn't appear to know this young maiden, or knew where she lived. But he appeared very satisfied that he had found Samson in their area. First and foremost, he was interested in the bounty that was on Samson's head. So, he left in a hurry.

However, Samson wasn't that concern. So, he continued his walk with this young maiden to her home. Yet, in his mind, he knew that the officers of the Gazites would be very glad when they get the news that he was in their town. For in their mind, him being in the town of Gaza, they knew they had their man.

Therefore, Samson was sure that as soon as the officer of the Gazites had gotten the news that he was in their town, they rushed and informed the lords of the Philistines that he had come into their town and they knew the area he was visiting.

He was also sure that after these officer of the Gazites had informed the lords of the Philistines, these officers of the Gazites hurried and covered the area with security guards where he had been seen.

Unquestionably, Samson knew that the Gazites were too afraid to confront him themselves. For they were clearly aware of what he could do to them. However, he knew that they would set up contingent squads to watch the whole area so that he could not escape.

He also knew that officers of the Gazites would also set up a team to watch over the area of his sighting until they could get more backup reinforcement to help at the gate. These officer of the Gazites were well aware that it would take many of them to subdue him.

Meanwhile, Samson's wisdom did tell him also that this suspicious man was indeed a spy. And that this spy did inform the officers of the Gazites who quickly put guards near the gate of the city to carefully watch for him as he attempted to leave their town in the early morning.

However, since the officers of the Gazites knew that Samson was in their area, they weren't so much interested in capturing him right away. They could wait until help from the lords of the Philistines come with their backup support.

Definitely, the officers of the Gazites were more concerned about Samson escaping passed the gate with the crowds in the early morning light. Hence, they wanted to keep track of his general location while the darkness covers the land.

Truly, the Scripture strongly concurred, "And it was told the Gazites, saying, Samson is come hither. And they compassed him in, and laid wait for him all night in the gate of the city, and were quiet all the night, saying, In the morning, when it is day, we shall kill him" (Judges 16:2).

Unquestionably, they had hoped that when he walked to the gate to leave their town in early morning, they would kill him. But Samson was well aware of their perceived intentions and he knew what he was going to do. So, he walked all the way to this maiden's home without showing any concern.

Samson's One-Night Stand in Gaza

# CHAPTER 21

# Romancing With Philistine Maiden

Meanwhile, Samson jubilantly accompanied this young maiden to her home. Despite the suspicious man who more than likely turned out to be a spy, he was not going to miss this euphoric opportunity to enjoy his gorgeous date for tonight.

After they had walked about three blocks from where they had met, they arrived to her home. On first glance, Samson was thoroughly impressed. For he found her home to be a beautiful little decorative flat. And her little distinctively sophisticated flat was in the center of the complex attached to a group of other ornamental stylish homes.

Delightfully, when they had entered into her home, Samson felt completely at ease. For he was inundated with its decorated colors and its exotic sweet-scents. Indeed, as soon as he had entered the large living room, he could smell the sweet-smelling scent of a potent physically arousing perfume. Certainly, this delicate fragrance permeated the air and had the potency to greatly indulge the senses.

Charmingly, Samson was most impressed with the orderly and beautifully arrangement of her furniture. Gorgeous chairs, tables, and large oval wall mirrors were situated very nicely in this large living room, and they were immaculate. In fact, her home was gorgeously prepared for entertaining royalty.

However, after entering the room, this gorgeous maiden courteously asked Samson to sit while she quickly poured some warm water for him to take a bath. While she prepared the bath water, Samson looked all around this beautifully decorated living room and was in wonderment. He couldn't believe how this beautiful young maiden had prepared her home so brilliantly.

Afterward, she returned and took his hand and led him into the room to take his bath. The decoration and ambiance of this room left him speechless. In fact, the bathtub was made for kings. Then, she said, "My dear gentleman, please prepare to get into the tub."

After Samson had gotten into the tub, she gently and delicately washed his back and shoulders while he washed himself in the tub. After he had finished with his bath, she graciously led him to her bedroom. Then, she asked him to lie down on her soft bed until she returned. This bed had been made from Down feather and it was very comfortable.

Quickly, she left him to go into another room to change into something more comfortable. And when she returned to the bedroom a few minutes later, this young maiden was a bundle of beauty and loveliness. She had changed to a flaunting cutout black mini dress that was made out of a thin layer of pleasurable silk.

Indeed, this gorgeous maiden was indeed the darling little angel that he had hope to meet when he left his home. She was dazzlingly attractive to him from head to toe. She had the smell of the sweetest rose. And he was ravished by her beauty.

Then, with a huge glamorous smile, she came up to him and softly placed herself into his arms. And with her eyes moisture with romance, she looked up to him and whispered, "My love, I am all yours tonight! Take me, I am your baby until the morning light."

And as Samson looked on her with great desire, she whispered to him, "My heart feels the richness of your loving attraction for me. Darling pleased take me beyond the blissful shores of your affection. And carry me to that indescribable height of heavenly passion springing from your efficacious strength and desire." She also had fallen for him even though she was a woman of the street.

Of course, Samson was very delighted to hear those words, for the tenor of those words sweetly filled his heart with great desire. And he agreed quickly! Then, he took her in his arms. And with the strength of a man who knew the power of love, he warmly embraced her with his tender romantic squeeze.

Quickly, she held fast to him in total surrender. And with the joy of passion, he amorously serenaded this gorgeous maiden across the blissful oasis of romance to the heavenly paradise of pleasing ecstasy. In so doing, she was brought to the mountaintop of euphoric pleasure, a romantic adventure she had not experienced before.

Truly, this young Philistine's maiden was thoroughly caressed in the tenderness of pleasing love. So much so, that this young maiden became intensely thrilled with Samson's extraordinary ability to bring her to the delight of womanhood.

And unexpectantly, her heart felt for Samson in such a way that she didn't want him to go away. Indeed, she did not want him to leave her. Even though they had only met for a night, she wanted him to be with her forever. But he could not commit to her in that way. He knew that in the mystery of the night, the murderous intention of the Gazites was waiting for him.

<br />

## CHAPTER 22
# A Midnight Escape From the Gazites

Unquestionably, Samson knew that the officers of the Gazites would be anxiously waiting for him. Therefore, he knew that he had to make a daring escape for his life. Despite enjoying rapturous delight with this gorgeous Philistine maiden, he was well aware that he could not overstay his visit with her.

So, around midnight, he knew that it was time for him to leave the home of this beautiful maiden and put into effect his getaway. He had immensely enjoyed his visit with this delightful young maiden in Gaza, but the time had come for him to spoil the expectations of these vicious avengers.

Therefore, as this stunning young maiden held on to him with tears flowing from her eyes, he arose and carefully started toward the door of her home. As she held fast to him, he gently kissed her cheeks and attempted to open the door of her home.

Obviously, this innocent maiden had no idea that this man Samson, whom she had just met, had been observed by a spy from the officers of the Gazites. And he had not informed her of their suspected spying on him.

Therefore, not knowing why the man whom she had quickly fallen in love with was leaving so suddenly, she felt very hurt that he had decided not to spend the night with her. Indeed, she was very puzzled why he had to leave so soon.

As indicated earlier, the Scripture clearly stated, "Then went Samson to Gaza, and saw there an harlot, and went in unto her" (Judges 16:1).

However, after Samson had opened the door to go away, this beautiful maiden cried out to him, "Darling, please don't go! My dear, please stay longer! My heart wishes for you to stay longer." Hearing this, Samson picked her up and held her close to his heart.

Then, he whispered, "My sweet love, you have brought much joy to my heart. And I have enjoyed your precious love immensely. But the time has come that I must go away. And I cannot stay here any longer."

Quickly, with both arms wrapped tightly around his neck, she cried out again, "Darling, if you must go, please promise me that you will come and visit with me again very soon. My heart reaches out to you!"

Samson smiled pleasingly, for he knew that this gorgeous Philistine maiden had fallen for him. Then, he gently put her down and kissed her forehead. And with a warm heart, he quickly gave her the sweetheart promise. Afterward, with a purposeful walk, he started toward the gate.

Cautiously, as he walked, he scanned the area very thoroughly to get an impression where the suspected guards of the Gazites could be hiding. Clearly, he was convinced that the spy had described him to the officers of the Gazites. And he was sure they had gathered in large numbers.

Therefore, he meticulously left the area while it was still early and too dark for the officers of the Gazites to notice him. And he had prepared himself to walk passed the guards undetected. Yet, he knew that he had the advantage for there were many persons leisurely going back and forth throughout the town.

<br />

Definitely, he knew that the officers of the Gazites were not aware of his exact location and didn't know exactly where he had gone. They also didn't know the young maiden whom he had been seen with. So, they didn't exactly know how to plan his whereabouts.

In fact, these officers of the Gazites had no idea when he would be leaving or where he would be coming from. But they knew that he was in Gaza. So, their best hope was to catch him when he comes to the gate in early morning.

And since it was only midnight, there were only a few guards watching inattentively about fifty yards from the gate. They weren't expecting him to arrive until the early morning. Therefore, Samson carefully walked passed the guards and slowly pushed forward to the powerfully strong gate with two doors.

And when he approached the gate, he found it securely locked. Therefore, he decided to teach a lesson to those few guards who were watching the gate inattentively. For he didn't need the doors to be opened to make his getaway. Quickly, he decided to move the two doors and the gate themselves.

Miraculously, with God's help, Samson quietly took the doors of the gate of the city, and the two posts, and put them upon his shoulders. Then, he went away with them. He took the bar and all. In fact, he carried the gate of the city and the two posts up to the top of a hill in Hebron, some forty miles away.

In truth, the Scripture declared, "And Samson lay till midnight, and arose at midnight, and took the doors of the gate of the city, and the two posts, and went away with them, bar and all, and put them upon his shoulders, and carried them up to the top of an hill that is before Hebron" (Judges 16:3).

However, when the sun began to rise over the land, the officers of the Gazites and the inattentive guards were terribly surprised. For neither did the officers of the Gazites nor the guards see or hear Samson leave the area. In fact, the officers of the Gazites thought he was still in their town.

But when these officers of the Gazites and the inattentive guards turned and walked toward the gate to see Samson standing at the gate, they couldn't believe what they saw. Instantly, they were thrown out of their wits, for they saw no standing gate.

Then, they knew that Samson had slipped passed them and their inattentive guards. For instead of a gate with two doors standing tall, they saw a wide opened area with a big hole in the ground. And they knew that Samson was the only one who could do such a thing.

Certainly, the doors of the gate and the two posts were gone. Instead, a big hole was left for the officers of the Gazites and the inattentive guards to ponder. And the curious spy had also lost his bounty as well. For the replacement of the gate and the two doors were more than what the bounty was worth.

Immediately, the officers of the Gazites and the spy looked toward each other with great disgust and anger. For they felt greatly humiliated that Samson had outwitted them again! Indeed, the man in whom they thought they had cornered, had slipped away from them again. And he was now safely somewhere in the protection of his people.

## CHAPTER 23
# *Safely Returns Home to his People*

Miraculously, with God's help, Samson had escaped the murderous intentions of the officers of the Gazites and the lords of the Philistines. And in his daring escape from their clutches in Gaza, he took the doors of the gate and the two posts of which these vicious men had hoped would aid them in his capture.

Definitely, Samson knew that these brutal and cruel men had depended on these two huge gates to aid them in their surprise attack. So, he took their weapon of offence far away from them. And it would take some time and money for the Gazites to restore their gates and secure their little town as before.

And with those two huge gates missing, the comfort and safety of the town of Gaza would be disrupted for some time. Hence, he wanted to punish the officers of the Gazites and the lords of the Philistines severely for their continued harassment of him.

Certainly, these Philistines' leaders had wanted to avenge Samson for the killing of their people. So, they tried everything they could do to catch him off guard. For they had hope that they could track him down and kill him. Now, he had given them more anger to add to their list.

Unquestionably, Samson was very pleased with the revenge he had given to the officers of the Gazites. And he was trusting in the Lord to protect him, for he was following his leading. He knew that every conflict he had with the leaders of the Philistines was the result of his miraculous calling to defeat them. He knew that it was God's grace that had brought him this far.

Without doubt, Samson knew that he was making these great escapes and doing these fantastic feats because of the Lord's help. He knew that God was using him to overthrow the domination of the Philistines through his superhuman strength. For he had been born for that purpose.

Thanks to God! After miraculously escaping the deadly intentions of the officers of the Gazites, Samson had safely returned home to the protection of his own people. In fact, he had escaped their fierce anger secured and unharmed with his life. Although his people in Israel were not aware of what he had just experienced, he had returned home and was carefully performing his duties as judge over them.

Certainly, in reflection, Samson felt that Gaza was a lovely little town, and he had enjoyed his visit there. Truly, he had begun to develop strong feelings for the precious little Philistine maiden whom he had met. But he knew that he could not visit her or her town anymore. And he did not want to endanger the peace and security of this innocent young maiden at all.

Meanwhile, being the judge and deliverer of Israel, Samson recognized that he was genuinely loved by his people. He had now been Israel's judge for more that nineteen years. And the people of Israel were experiencing great peace and quietness away from the Philistine's domination.

Undoubtedly, Samson saw the great love his people had for him and he didn't want to disturb their peace. For some of the women would shed tears when he slipped away from them. Although he wasn't completely sure why he was continually upsetting his people in making these daring visits into the Philistines' areas, he concluded that these visits were of the Lord.

Certainly, he was well aware that his daring ventures into the Philistine areas made his people very nervous. And he wanted his people to enjoy his judgeship and feel safety for him. Therefore, he decided to suspend his travels into the areas of the Philistines for a while.

Absolutely, the people of Israel were finally enjoying quietness in their lives. They could now go out and enjoy their lives without the Philistines interfering with them. In fact, they no longer had to worry about harassment when they walk up and down the street in their areas.

Nevertheless, most of all, Samson wanted to give the officers of the Gazites and the lords of the Philistines some time to recover from their disappointment in not capturing him in Gaza. He knew that his daring escape from the officers of the Gazites and those inattentive guards left them wondering how could they capture this strongman called Samson.

Unquestionably, he also knew that the officers of the Gazites and the lords of the Philistines were now on heavy alert looking for him. In addition to the killing of their people, they were determined to take vengeance on him for what he had done to their two doors and the gate. Clearly, he knew the grave danger of him venturing again into their land.

Obviously, Samson had now accepted the fact that he was a wanted man throughout the land of the Philistines. And he was fully aware that retaliatory orders had been issued against him for his capture and arrest. So, he decided to suspend his travel to that land until this boiling retaliatory tension against him cool down.

# CHAPTER 24

## Travels to the Valley of Sorek

Definitely, Samson suspended his travels to the land of the Philistines. In fact, it was a while before he gave any serious thoughts to returning to that land. For he knew that at every gate there would be guards watching for him. And with the bounty placed on him, he knew that these guards would not hesitate to take drastic measure to capture him as soon as he walked through the gate.

However, despite all of the threats and the efforts put forth by the lords of the Philistines to capture and kill him, there were curious feelings still stirring up in him. It was as if he was being compelled to go again to their land. He could not get free from these curious urges to confront the Philistines.

Indeed, through several strange and mysterious visions, he now perceived that the Spirit of God was moving upon him to continue the deliverance mission in which he had been called. He was to continue the overthrow of the domination of the Philistines.

Even though he was now the judge of Israel, he was well aware that he had also been called to begin the deliverance of Israel from the domination from the Philistines. And the only way for him to defeat the Philistines he had to be in contact with them in their land.

Besides, he was also getting an unquenchable urge to go back to the town of Timnath where he met his precious Philistine wife. Even though she was now gone, he vividly remembered the strong feelings he had for this first love. He also joyfully remembered the beautiful young maiden he had met in Gaza. For both of these beautiful maidens left fond memories in his heart.

Undeniably, Samson greatly loved the beautiful young ladies of the Philistine people. And he deeply missed the spirited excitement of socializing with these beautiful Philistine maidens in their own land. For they indeed brought pleasure and excitement to his heart.

Clearly, there was something delightfully pleasing in being in the company of those gorgeous Philistine maidens. Their modesty and seemingly innocent personality brought splendid joy to his heart. Without doubt, those women of the Philistines had become a romantic obsession to him.

However, being consciously aware of the intense manhunt the lords of the Philistines had put in operations to capture him, he was fully aware that he could not visit the same place twice. Certainly, he remembered those two Philistine towns he had visited, and how his presence in those two towns had sparked a violent and destructive end.

Now, he knew that he could not travel again to those towns where the search for him had developed into a network of house to house surveillance. For he was very cognizant that if he was to return to the land of the Philistines and travel into those areas he had already visited, he would see his name and photo posted on every most wanted sign throughout their area. And the leaders in those towns would be on high alert for his capture.

Without doubt, Samson knew that he would be easily recognized. For all of the people of the Philistines had heard of him, the strong man of Israel. And the bounty placed on his head would be very attractive for anyone to enjoy. So, in order for him to fulfill his desire to return to the land of the Philistine, he had to be willing to take the risk.

However, despite all the risks involved in returning to the Philistine area, Samson decided to venture into a place where he felt was relatively safe. In fact, he decided to travel to a place not too far from Zorah and Eshtaol, the place of his youth. Although he knew that since this place was a Philistine town, the lords of the Philistines would be there as well.

Meanwhile, after several months of being away from the land of the Philistines, he decided to return. This time, he wanted to go to the valley of Sorek. This valley borders with Dan and the Philistines. This place was also not too far away from Gaza.

Therefore, despite the people of Israel's objection, he started this risky journey to the valley of Sorek. He had hoped to enter into this valley town quietly and make quiet peace with the people of this border town. He had also hoped to meet a beautiful young maiden in this valley town.

Strangely, he arrived at this place very early in the morning and he was surprised. For he wasn't immediately noticed when he entered this sleepy valley. Nevertheless, since this place was a border town, he felt a little more secure. In fact, after a few days, he began to venture slowly to the people of the marketplace.

He loved this town and wanted to spend some time here. Even though he was still the judge of Israel, he began to spend much of his time in this valley of Sorek. He was very pleased that he was able to move about with very little notice.

Indeed, when he walked up and down their streets, no one seemed to know or care that he was Samson, the strong man of Israel. He was just another tourist who was trying to survive and enjoy the town. And he was enjoying his contacts with the beautiful maidens of Sorek.

However, he was still very conscious of the lords of the Philistines. They wanted him captured and dead. So, in all honesty, he was not going to let his guards down. Despite being accepted in this valley town of Sorek, he knew the Lords of the Philistines would not forget what he had done to thousands of their people.

Samson Meets Delilah in Sorek

# CHAPTER 25

# Meets and Falls for the Ruse of Delilah

Definitely, Samson had discovered his oasis of joy and excitement. For he was blissfully enjoying the company of many of these beautiful Philistine maidens in this valley town of Sorek. And he was experiencing intense pleasure and fun reveling with these beautiful angels of love.

Undeniably, these beautiful young maidens in this valley town were very responsive to him in every way. And they all seemed to be very delighted and pleased to be in his company. Therefore, despite his judgeship in Israel, Samson decided to make this valley town his second home.

In truth, Samson was having fun with one or more of these beautiful maidens each single day. And his carousing with these attractive maidens of joy seemed to have no end. But then, his eye caught sight of another gorgeous young maiden who appeared different from all of the other maidens.

Clearly, he could not resist staring toward this extraordinarily attractive young maiden. She had that exotic appeal which was indeed very charming. Indeed, this young maiden was totally and utterly glamorous.

Unquestionably, Samson couldn't wait to introduce himself to her, for her beauty seemed to jump out to him. Apart from the other attractive maidens, his heart felt the need to devote some of his time with her. So, he approached this attractive young maiden with his most fearless confidence.

In fact, he walked up to her and introduced himself. He said, "My name is Samson, and who do I have the pleasure in talking with? What is your name?" She looked firmly toward him and was pleasantly surprised.

Then, she smiled admiringly and said, "Oh, you are Samson! I have heard a lot about you. And I had wanted to meet you. My name is Delilah. I am pleased to make my acquaintance with you. Are you enjoying yourself?"

Samson quickly replied, "Yes, I am. But it could be more fun if you would give me the opportunity to know you." She responded, "Please, go ahead. Please tell me more about you!" Then, he joined with her in conversation.

Indisputably, this Philistine's maiden was very beautiful. She was also very intelligent and elegant. She had those exceptional qualities that Samson had desired in a woman. Her eyes sparkle, and her mannerism was adoringly sweet. To him, it was love at first sight. But she was a woman with duplicity and Samson felt for her deception.

Certainly, Delilah loved Samson's bold and strong masculinity. And they began to show promising interest in each other. Actually, she was very pleased to be with him. And Samson began to spend more time with her. In fact, his love grew more and more for her. Indeed, she was given him a lot of fun. But she had hope for gain.

However, in a relative short period of time, Samson fell deeply in love with her. In fact, he was smitten by her wile, and she became the only Philistine maidens whom he wanted to spend time with. But he had forgotten the advice and warning his father had given to him.

Unquestionably, he wasn't very careful in his disclosure to this new love. Since he felt at ease with her, he trusted her. And his love for her blinded him from her wile. And he began to share with her everything about his life.

Apart from her beauty, Delilah was different from the other maidens. For she used men for her advantage, and she was prone to extract money (or anything profitable) from them. She was akin to our modern day "gold-digger".

Nevertheless, Samson was enamored with her. And he felt that because he loved her, she loved him with the same amount of care. He didn't know that she could express great affection without love. Therefore, he began to confide to her some very private information.

In fact, he disclosed to her how he was being mistreated by the lords of the Philistines. He also said that he didn't trust them. And he was careful not to be seen by them. Then, he told her that the lords of the Philistines hated him and were after him to kill him.

As she looked toward him with a perplexed look, he also declared to her how God had helped him in giving superhuman strength. And he was able to defend himself when thousands of their soldiers tried to attack him.

After hearing those words, Delilah knew that there was something different about Samson. She saw that he was very brave and daring, but he had great distrust for the lords of the Philistines. Indeed, he had also convinced her that he felt deeply threatened by them. And he felt very unsafe when they were around.

But she didn't know what he meant by superhuman strength. And she didn't know what he meant when he said that his God had helped him. But she had learned by his behavior that he would be on high alert any time he felt that the lords of the Philistines were near him. And he was always on the lookout for them.

Even though Delilah had not seen the lords of the Philistines, she trusted Samson's disclosures of them in his apprehensions. She knew that he would leap into action to defend himself the moment he realized they were near him. Therefore, she began to think how she could use his anxiety and fears to her advantage.

# CHAPTER 26
# *Delilah Recruited by the Philistines*

Meanwhile, the news began to spread that Samson, the strongman of Israel, was now living in the valley of Sorek. In fact, this news traveled very quietly all over the area. Ultimately, this news made it all the way to the lords of the Philistines.

And when those Philistine leaders found out that Samson had indeed returned to their land, they were immediately pleased. For they had waited a long time for him to return. Now, they needed to know the place he was living in their area so that they could capture him.

Indeed, these angry leaders of the Philistines sought very hard to locate where he was living. And when they learned that he was spending time with a Philistine maiden named Delilah, they quickly sought to know who she was, and to locate her place of residence.

Quickly, they learned that Delilah was a prominent resident of the valley of Sorek. They also learned that she was a woman of great intelligence and could be approachable for gain. And to their surprise, they also discovered that Samson had established residence with her. Now, they believed that this time they would capture this man and kill him.

Therefore, they quickly conspired among themselves to ask this maiden Delilah to help them find the secret of Samson's great strength. They also decided to offer her a huge amount of money to work for them. Hence, they all agreed to offer her money.

Readily, they all believe that since this maiden Delilah was a Philistine, she would not object to their offer. So, without hesitation, the lords of the Philistines came unto her home. However, before knocking, they looked very carefully to be sure that Samson was not around. They didn't want any contact with him until they could be assured of victory,

Strangely, on this morning, Samson happened to be away in Israel during some judgeship functions. And unbeknownst to the lords of the Philistines, he was expected to be returning to her home around midday.

However, with no sight of him, they quickly knocked on Delilah's door and stepped back. When she came to the door, they were immediately impressed. She appeared to be a lady of great promise. They carefully approached her and said, "Are you Delilah?"

She looked toward them with some concern and responded, "Yes, I am she. Why do you ask?"

Then, they said unto her, "Don't worry, we will cause you no harm. We are the lords of the Philistines. How are you today?"

Then, she looked toward them and thought hesitantly "lords of the Philistines". However, she responded, "I am fine, Thank you for asking! How can I help you?"

Of course, these lords of the Philistines caught her hesitancy and responded to her, "We are looking for a man named Samson. Do you know him?"

At this question, everything Samson had said to her about the lords of the Philistines flashed through her mind. Therefore, she responded very cautiously, "Yes, he is my friend. However, I have not seen him today. But he will be returning very soon."

Quickly, the leader of the Philistines answered, "We are so happy to speak to you. we have been looking for him. We want to know whether you can help us?"

After hearing this, Delilah knew that the lords of the Philistines were indeed after Samson. So, she quickly asked, "Ok, what type of help you need?"

They answered, "Samson is a great defender of Israel, and he is such a strong man. He has destroyed many of us. And we don't know where his great strength comes from. Can you find out what is the source of his great strength?"

Since Samson had told her that the lords of the Philistines wanted to capture him, she thought maybe there was something in it for her. Therefore, she replied, "Ok, I will do what I can to help. I know my dear friend Samson is stronger than any other man. But he has not told me what makes him so strong. It seemed to be between him and his God. Anyway, I will ask him and get back to you."

When the lords of the Philistines heard her response, they could not believe she would talk to them so calmly about Samson. Therefore, they quickly made her aware of the offer they had agreed to give her for her help.

With great promise, they said to her, "Entice him, and see wherein his great strength lieth, and by what means we may prevail against him, that we may bind him to afflict him; and we will give thee every one of us eleven hundred pieces of silver" (Judges 16:5).

Immediately, when Delilah heard of the amount of money the lords of the Philistines were offering to her, she quickly agreed to help them. Despite knowing that Samson greatly admired her and love her, she was very excited to get this lucrative offer from the lords of the Philistines.

Although she loved Samson and admired him for his great strength, her love for the money was just too strong. And this large amount of money was more than several years of her labor. She could not say no.

So, she decided that she would help the lords on the Philistines find the secret of Samson's strength. And she would take the money. Of course, she was fully aware that, despite being a Philistine and identified with those whom Samson had killed, her actions were unwarranted and it would be an gross act of betrayal. For she knew that Samson sincerely loved her.

Therefore, regardless of Samson's feelings for her, she felt that she needed to help her people and gained the money that was offered. Hence, she decided to entice him to learn where did his great strength come from. Also, she had intended to use his anxiety and fears of the lords of the Philistines against him to get him to reveal his strength secret.

Delilah Entices in Deception

# CHAPTER 27

# Entices Samson with Treachery

Undeniably, Delilah quickly agreed to accept this lucrative offer of the lords of the Philistines wholeheartedly. Indeed, after hearing this very valuable offer they had proposed to her, she did not hesitate in accepting this profitable reward money. And she only had to find the source of Samson's great strength.

Certainly, she had agreed with the lords of the Philistines to get it as soon as possible. So, she had asked them to wait in her chamber. And when Samson came home and revealed the source of his strength to her, they would be able to grab him right away.

Immediately, all of the lords of the Philistines agreed with her and decided to wait. They also promised to have someone waiting in the chamber every day until Samson revealed to her the source of his great strength.

Unfortunately, despite all of the love and honesty Samson had shown to Delilah, she was willing to do whatever the lords of the Philistines wanted to get this rewarding offer. She knew that this money would go a long way with her. And in no uncertain terms, she was willing to sacrifice his life for the money.

Definitely, regardless of the feelings and emotions she had to betray, Delilah was not going to miss this opportunity to make some well needed money. She had already realized how long it would take her to earn this amount of money working in the fields.

Irrefutably, she had decided to do whatever was required to satisfy the lords of the Philistines. Indeed, she had decided to express her sensuality in such a way to Samson so that he would open up to her. Even though she knew that her actions would betray him, she took comfort in the fact that she wasn't going to do any physical harm to him herself.

Therefore, despite knowing how strongly Samson disliked and distrusted the Philistines, she had decided to get this profitable reward from them no matter how long it took. Hence, she quietly put her deception into motion.

Certainly, she was thoroughly convinced that Samson loved and cared for her. And she knew that he greatly admired her and wanted to be with her. Therefore, she felt within herself that it wouldn't take long for her to get him to reveal the source of his great strength.

So, before he had arrived to her home from his travel, she prepared herself to greet him in her most enticing way. Hence, she decided to put on one of her most revealing and appealing outfits, the outfit he really loved. She knew he would be overcome with the sultriness and seductiveness of her physical appearance.

Therefore, as soon as Samson returned to her home, she rushed up to him and gave him an affectionate embrace. Then, she kissed him excitedly and crawled into his arms. And with deep affection, she whispered to him very tenderly, "Darling, I missed you. What took you so long to return? I was so worried about you!"

Quickly, Samson responded to her, "Darling, I was delayed along the way by a couple groups of hostile men who tried to attack me. But I defended myself with the help of the Lord." However, he didn't tell her that those two groups of hostile men were her people.

Immediately, Delilah stared toward him and expressed great excitement. She was convinced that he had defeated two groups of aggressive and boisterous men. So, she said to him, "Oh, you are so brave! You are the man who can protect me!"

Then, she thought, "Oh Dear, after all of that fisticuffs you must be tired! Please take a quick bath and lie down. I will give you a massage." She wanted him to become very comfortable so that he could reveal to her all that she would ask him.

And with great excitement, as soon as he had taken his bath, they both got in bed together. Then, as they lay together, she snuggled up to him and kissed him passionately. Affectionately, she began to glowingly admire his ability to defend himself against those groups of unfriendly men.

Of course, the conversation slowly turned to his muscular physique. She even complimented him for being much stronger than any other man. She even shared with him her fascination with his stamina and strength.

She was lavishing him with his sense of self hoping that he was closely paying attention to her generous compliments. And she was hoping that he was being persuaded by her caring and unselfish admiration of his masculinity. But he merely lay there with just a few words.

However, when Delilah saw that Samson was not responding in the way she wanted him to, she rolled on top of him and straddled him to sensually tease him. Then, she put her left hand in his right hand and her right hand in his left hand, and smiled toward him in a seductive manner.

Then, she said in her most enticing voice, "My dear Samson, you have such big arms and shoulders, you are so strong. And you are not afraid of gangs and posse. You are not even afraid of lions and wild animals. In fact, you have defended yourself against whole armies. Please tell me, I beg you. where is all of this strength coming from? Darling, if someone wanted to bound you to defeat you, how could they do it?"

Even though Samson had no knowledge of Delilah's recent contact with the lords of the Philistines, he sensed right away that the one he loved was not being herself today. Indeed, he felt that her conversation was leading up to something. She was not being the cute, demure young maiden that he knew.

In fact, he perceived the impatience in her voice and knew that there was more to her question than just the idea of his strength. He had learned her affectionate behavior when she needed him to hold her. But her romantic behavior today was much too planned. It also appeared a little too premature.

So, he responded to her in a way to satisfy her curiosity. Because he greatly loved her, he didn't want to be abrupt and hurt her feelings. He wanted her to feel comfort with him being different from other men.

Therefore, he tried to give his precious love something that would make her think. He was hoping that she would not push the subject any deeper. He knew why he was super strong and it was from God for Israel's deliverance. And He knew that God still had more work for him to do.

# CHAPTER 28
# *Samson Evades Strength Secret*

Without doubt, Delilah was desperately looking forward toward the reward money. Nevertheless, she was also very eager to hear what Samson would describe as his strength source. Therefore, even though still straddled on top of him, she quickly stopped her sensual teasing to listen very carefully to his explanation of his strength source. In fact, she looked expectantly into his eyes.

Definitely, Samson saw the deep attention she was giving to him as he spoke. So, he looked up to her and said, "If they bind me with seven green bowstrings that were never dried, then shall I be weak, and be as another man." He honestly thought that she would be overwhelmed with the unbreakable strength of cords and bowstrings.

Quickly, without probing into what he had said to her, Delilah considered that Samson was telling her the truth. And she was immediately excited. For his response to his strength source sounded good to her. Therefore, she felt in herself, I have gotten the answer I needed, for he had revealed to me his strength source.

Then, she quickly stopped her romantic preludes to take care of an emergency. However, she left quietly and delivered this information to the waiting Philistines. And this information was passed on to the lords of the Philistines who were amazed and very pleased. In fact, they couldn't believe that she had gotten this crucial information so quickly.

Certainly, the lords of the Philistines rushed to get the seven green bowstrings. And within a short while, they returned with the seven green bowstrings which had not been dried. They immediately gave them to her. For they knew these cords could not be broken by any ordinary man. This time, they were sure that they had their man.

Quickly, Delilah asked Samson to allow her to bind him. He was surprised that she had gotten those seven green bowstrings so fast. Anyway, he allowed her to bind him. He didn't know what else she was going to do. He was hoping that this deep curiosity of his strength source would end soon.

Thus, as soon as Delilah had bound him with those seven green bowstrings, she thought now that this huge amount of reward money is certainly mine. Of course, there were trained men of the Philistines lying in wait, abiding with her in the chamber waiting on the signal from her to spring in.

Therefore, after she had thoroughly bind Samson, she tried to intimidate him. In fact, she used his own alertness and apprehensions of the lord of the Philistines against him. She said very suddenly, "Samson, the lords of the Philistines are here coming after you!"

She knew those words would get his attention. But Samson stood up immediately and broke the bowstrings as a thread of tow is broken when it toucheth the fire. It happened so fast that it caused Delilah to jump back. So, the source of his strength was not known.

However, when Delilah saw Samson's quick reaction in breaking the bowstrings, she was very disappointed with him. For the source of his great strength had not been revealed. In fact, he had broken the bowstrings with ease, and he had not told her the truth about his strength source. She felt he had played a trick on her in some way.

Therefore, she said unto him very firmly, "Ok Samson, you are having fun with me today. You did get me with that one trick. Now, let's be serious, and stop leading me on. Darling, I am begging you, where do you get this great strength? How can someone bound you?"

This time, Samson knew his love Delilah was honestly seeking to know the source of his great strength. For he saw the bitter disappointment in her eyes. And he felt that she was also a little frustrated as well, for she thought no ordinary man could not break the green bowstrings. But he broke those seven green withs with ease. It was like they had been burned with fire.

However, after a few days, she asked him the second time. Then, he was thoroughly convinced that she really wanted to know what was the source of his strength. For she was becoming teary eyes. But he still didn't know why she was so seriously concerned about his strength source. And he surely didn't know that she was in direct contact with the lords of the Philistines.

So, he responded to her this time in a way that should satisfy her curiosity. In fact, he described to her a strength source that would be totally impossible for any ordinary man to do. It was an extreme test of strength, and he didn't think that she would follow up on this one. He said unto her, "If they tie me very securely with new ropes that had never been used, then I will be weak just like any other man."

Yet, this time Delilah was sure he was telling her the truth. And with his serious look, she believed him. Therefore, she took new ropes, and tied him very securely, with both hands tied behind his back. She knew that no ordinary man could escape being bound in this way.

Then, she began to taunt him with the intimidation of the Philistines again. She said unto him with great excitement, "Samson, the lords of the Philistines are here coming after you!" Of course, there were men of the Philistines waiting in the chamber. And they were on edge that when the signal was given, they would come rushing in.

However, Samson stood up immediately and broke the new ropes from off his arms like a thread. He seemed to break these ropes and free himself effortlessly. This time, Delilah had gotten a little angry with him, for the ropes seem to magically break from his arms.

Then, she cried out to him with tears, "You are having a lot of fun again today. You got me with this one too! Why are you playing with me, and making me look foolish? This is the second time you have tricked me. Try being serious for a change! Where is all of this strength coming from? How can you be bound, please tell me? I want to know."

Seeing those deep emotions coming from Delilah, Samson knew that she had become very determined to get an answer that worked. Indeed, she was so resolved in finding the source of his great strength that she had lost all sense of decency and decorum. Yet, he did not know that she had colluded with the lords of the Philistines.

# CHAPTER 29
# *Delilah's Treachery Prevailed*

Undoubtedly, with the annoyed tone in Delilah's voice, Samson sensed now that her interest in the source of his great strength was more than mere curiosity. And due to her utter frustration with not knowing his strength source, he knew that she was not going to give up easily in seeking the source of his great strength. And he was very perplexed why she was so vehement in wanting to know his strength source.

Without question, Samson still thought that Delilah loved and cared for him. For she was passionately sharing her love with him every day. However, he was blinded by his great love for her. For he had no idea that the one he loved was daily keeping the lords of the Philistines abreast of his every move.

Nevertheless, because of his great love for her, he wanted to please her and make her happy. Indeed, he wanted her to settle down and be her sweet self again. So he said to her, "Ok, this time, I am going to give you the answer you are seeking for. Indeed, I am going to tell you the source of my great strength. I hope you will be satisfied and not ask me for it again."

With that promise made to Delilah, her expectation grew by leaps and bounds, she agreed right away not to pressure him again. After all, she thought this time he would tell her the truth. For this was her third attempt to get the information from him.

Definitely, she didn't want to keep the lords of the Philistines waiting much longer for the answer. For they might withdraw their lucrative money offer from her. So, she pleaded to Samson, "Darling, go on, pleased tell me!"

Then, as Delilah carefully observed, Samson put his hands through the seven locks of his hair and move them up and down and from side to side. With her eyes well focus on his every move, he said, "If you would take the seven locks of my head and twisted them all together with a pin to the beam, I will be no different than any other man."

When Delilah realized what he had just said, she was very pleased. For this testing method sounded very difficult and also very painful. And she thought that this was a good way to test his strength for she believed no ordinary man could do this. Hence, she thought Samson had finally told her the secret of his strength.

Therefore, as soon as Samson had fallen asleep, she quickly fastened the seven locks of his head with the pin. With this test of his strength, she was trembling with excitement. For she thought she had at last gotten the secret of his great strength.

Then, she woke Samson up and began to taunt him again. She said with great confidence, "Samson, the lords of the Philistines are here coming to get you!" And Samson awakened out of his sleep, and went away with the pin of the beam and the web. For this time, he was expecting her to do exactly what he had suggested to her.

However, with this tremendous show of strength and pain endurance, Delilah felt totally outdone and humiliated. For she thought he had finally told her the secret of his strength. But instead, he had fooled her again. And she didn't know what to tell the lords of the Philistines today. For she was really convinced.

Indeed, when Samson stood up and carried away the pin of the beam, and the web with the seven locks of his head, she was dumbfounded. For she still didn't know where his great strength was coming from. She knew now that she had to do something very different if she expected to get the answer. For the lords of the Philistines were waiting on her, and they were becoming impatient.

Therefore, she thought she would test Samson's love for her. In fact, she looked him straight in his eyes and said with moisture eyes, "Samson, how can you say, I love you, when you don't take me seriously? You don't have any love in your heart for me. I thought we were closer than that."

As Delilah thought about what she had said to him, she continued, "You haven't done anything but made fun of me these three times. And you have not told me where your great strength is coming from. I have been good to you, and have given you all of my love. Why are you treating me this way? Am I still your sweet love?" Then, her tears began to flow profusely.

However, with all of her generous affection toward him, Samson was not fully confident of her motives. By now, he was beginning to feel that all this intense affection shown to him must have a darker side. Yet, he still didn't know that she was driving him for an answer, for there was a huge amount of money waiting for her.

Nevertheless, with no positive news for the lords of the Philistines, Delilah knew that she had to get the answer soon. Therefore, she began to earnestly pressure Samson with her words. She persistently cried and begged him, showering him with love and tears. In fact, she enticed him in every way possible, dressing provocatively each and every day for him.

After a while, she began to wear Samson down, and he couldn't take her crying and begging any more. She was begging and pleading him all the time. So much so, that he had started to get very frustrated. Finally, he had become completely stressed out even unto death.

Even though he didn't know why she needed to know his strength source so badly, he thought that he would just go on and tell her because she was driving him to the grave. So, he decide to tell her the source of his strength.

In fact, he shared with her everything about his life. He told her about his Nazarite vow. He said, "I have been a Nazarite unto God from birth. And my hair is not to be cut. If my hair is cut, then my strength will go from me. And I will become weak like any other man."

In truth, the Scripture said, "And it came to pass, when she pressed him daily with her words, and urged him, so that his soul was vexed unto death; That he told her all his heart, and said unto her, There hath not come a razor upon mine head; for I have been a Nazarite unto God from my mother's womb: if I be shaven, then my strength will go from me, and I shall become weak, and be like any other man" (Judges 16:16-17).

Finally, Delilah realized that this revelation from Samson was what she had wanted to hear. She had waited for him to tell her all about his life. And when she realized that he had told her all his heart, she sent and called for the lords of the Philistines, saying, "Come up this once, for Samson hath shewed me all his heart."

In fact, when Delilah called for the lords of the Philistines, they noticed that the confident level of her voice had changed. This time she seemed very assured. And hearing this good news, they rushed up unto her. They trusted her judgment so much that they brought money in their hand. They felt this time she will get the source of his great strength. So, they began to wait.

# CHAPTER 30
# *Betrayed to the Philistines*

Certainly, this time Delilah was beside herself. She felt very confident that Samson had significantly opened up to her and told her his whole heart. In fact, she saw how intimate he had shared to her his personal soul. Truly, he did not leave out anything that could be told.

Definitely, in his sharing of the truth of his life, he told her all about his Nazarite vow to God. And in his description of its sacredness, he had revealed to her the source of his strength. He had said that in this Nazarite vow, he was never to cut his hair. For his obedience and faithfulness to the truth of this Nazarite vow demonstrated his faith in God. So, in his faithfulness and obedience to God, his hair had never been cut.

Indeed, at this time, his hair had grown to more than twenty inches in length. And he had braided his hair into seven locks. Yet, he did not tell her that he had been born to defeat the lords of the Philistines with his great strength.

Therefore, after learning about this Nazarite vow of his hair, Delilah knew why Samson's hair was so long. She was also convinced that his hair was the symbol of his strength. She was also completely aware that he was very faithful to his God.

Now, having this knowledge, she had to come up with a way to cut his hair without him knowing it. For Samson's long hair was his obedience to God. Meantime, she also treacherously shared this revelation of his Nazarite vow to the lords of the Philistines.

After getting this information, these enemies of Samson knew that there was some truth to this revelation of his Nazarite vow. For they had noticed that his hair was longer than any other man. Therefore, they quietly assembled with great speed into her chamber.

There, these vicious men cautiously waited for her to call them after his hair had been cut. They had great hope that today would be the day when this killer of their people would be captured.

Unquestionably, as these vicious enemies of Samson waited in Delilah's chamber, she began her treacherous sensual deceptive caressing of Samson's affection. And in her tender and deceiving cuddling and warmness, she gently created in Samson a pleasing and relaxing environment whereby he fell fast asleep upon her knees.

Then, she quickly called for the barber whom she had notified in advance. She quietly instructed him to carefully shaved off the seven locks of his hair. She wanted the barber to cut close to his head but not touch his head so that he would not wake up. Indeed, Samson slept all the while his hair was being cut.

However, as soon as Samson's hair had been cut off, Delilah was certain she had accomplished her goal. Therefore, she immediately woke him up and began to taunt him as she had done three times previously.

In fact, she spoke to him with supreme confidence, "Samson, the lords of the Philistines are here coming to get you!" Although she knew that this time it would be different, she was expecting him to get up and do something to demonstrate his great strength. But it didn't happen!

However, when Samson awoke out of his sleep, he said, "I will go out as at other times before, and shake myself." Because his hair had been cut, he had disobeyed his God and had lost the faith. But he wasn't aware that the Lord had left him.

Nevertheless, as soon as Samson tried to invoke the presence of God, he realized that He had departed from him. Tragically, through his disobedience in breaking the Nazarite vow, his supernatural strength had also gone from him as well.

Indeed, the Scripture said, "And when Delilah saw that he had told her all his heart, she sent and called for the lords of the Philistines, saying, Come up this once, for he hath shewed me all his heart. Then the lords of the Philistines came up unto her, and brought money in their hand. And she made him sleep upon her knees; and she called for a man, and she caused him to shave off the seven locks of his head; and she began to afflict him, and his strength went from him. And she said, The Philistines be upon thee, Samson. And he awoke out of his sleep, and said, I will go out as at other times before, and shake myself. And he wist not that the LORD was departed from him" (Judges 16:18-20).

Immediately, seeing Samson did not have the power and was no longer a threat to them, Delilah knew that his strength source had to do with his hair. Therefore, she gave the signal and the lords of the Philistines rushed in to captured him.

And when the lords of the Philistines discovered that his supernatural strength had left him, and he could not defend himself in a powerful way as he had done before, they quickly bind him fast with ropes. They knew then that they had their man.

And as soon as Samson was completely bound, Delilah tried to hide her face from him. But he looked toward her in complete disbelief, for she was to be blamed. Sadly, he learned very quickly why she was so determined to know his strength source. Then, he remembered the caution of his father.

However, with complete mastery of Samson, the lords of the Philistines quickly gave Delilah the money. Despite treacherously betraying her lover, she was very pleased to take the money of his betrayal. Samson watched as Delilah took the money and he knew what her motives were.

Then, these Philistines' leaders decided not to kill Samson. But they gouged out his eyes so that he could not see. And after putting out his eyes, they brought him down to the town of Gaza. There, they bound him with fetters of brass and began to use him as you would do beasts of burden.

In fact, the lords of the Philistines had him pulling the grinding machine in the prison house as one of the oxen. To them, the fun had just begun. They had planned to humiliate him until they had become satisfied that he had paid for all the death and destruction he had done to their people and country. But they had no idea that God had more work for Samson to do. He wasn't finished with him yet.

Of course, when Samson's brethren and all the house of his father had heard the news that Samson had been caught by the lords of the Philistines, they were very heartbroken. They were also very sad that he had revealed to them the secret to his great strength. But they knew that God still had his eyes on him.

# CHAPTER 31

# *Humiliated in the Prison in Gaza*

Now, the lords of the Philistines were all filled with jubilation and exultation. And they were thoroughly rejoicing. With Samson, the archenemy and killer of their people subdued and under their control, they felt that they had captured the threat to their people. Hence, they did not have to fear this strong man anymore in destroying their people at will.

Actually, after pursuing Samson for a long time, they had now taken hold of this strongman and had put out his eyes. And they had captured the killer of their people and had him just where they wanted him to be. They were now convinced that this strongman could not pose any more threat to them.

Surely, after killing thousands of their people, the lords of the Philistines felt that this strongman Samson could not see them anymore to inflict that kind of casualty upon them again. So, despite his growing hair and strength, they had decided to mock this enemy of theirs at their own pleasure.

Definitely, after hurriedly taking Samson from the hands of Delilah and quickly binding him with fetters of brass, they brought him down to Gaza. And in Gaza, they knew they could do with him whatever they wanted with him. Therefore, they decided to mock him and use him to grind at the mill.

And not fearing his superpower any more, the lords of the Philistines quickly took the advantage of him. In fact, they mocked him without pity. Actually, because of Samson's growing strength, they decided to use him to do the work of the ox and the ass.

At this time, the lords of the Philistines did not see Samson anymore worthy to be treated as a human being. And now with his growing strength, he was now to them as one of their livestock. And he was going to suffer for all that he had done to their people.

Certainly, this strongman Samson without his sight, the lords of the lords of the Philistines were assured that this killer of their people was defenseless. Despite his growing hair, they assumed that since he could not see them anymore, he could no longer pose a threat to them.

Therefore, besides using him to grind at the mill, he was used as a beast of burden. In reality, at Gaza, he was used as the jackass to pull the plow. They had determined that him being the judge of Israel, his humiliation would also bring shame on his people.

And in so doing, they presented him before large crowds at carnivals and festivals to mock him. In fact, huge crowds would gather to see Samson perform fantastic feats that no other man could do. Even the little Philistine children would come out and witness this strong man demonstrates his great strength.

In a way, this was the lords of the Philistines' way of punishing all Israel for what Samson had done to them. They thought that he alone had completely destroyed their dominion over the people of Israel. And that he alone had dramatically killed thousands of their people. And he alone had done all of this for his people Israel.

Unquestionably, the lords of the Philistines felt that much had been accomplished in their capturing of him. And they had given credit to their god Dagon for delivering Samson into their hands. And they now feel that their god Dagon was more superior than any other gods.

Undeniably, the lords of the Philistines felt that Dagon their god had tremendously helped them to subdue this strong man and to bring him to their control. Their god is now to be appeased and worshipped for his deity.

In reality, all of the people of the Philistines credited their god Dagon for assisting them in conquering this killer of their people. Hence, they all believed that their god Dagon needed to be honored. Therefore, they waited in anticipation.

# CHAPTER 32
# *Performs Before the Jubilant Crowd*

Indeed, the lords of the Philistines felt very ecstatic over their dramatic capture of Samson. However, they had one major flaw in their assumption of the source of his strength. They didn't know the power of his God, and thought that his haircut had to be done only once.

Unfortunately, they could not make the connection between the loss of his strength in the removal of his hair and his faith and power in his Nazarite vow. Indeed, they were convinced that they had found the source of his strength by cutting off his hair. They also thought that if Samson could not see them, he could not harm them. But God was setting the stage for their defeat. He wanted to use Samson one more time.

Therefore, as time went on, the hair of Samson's head grew long again. And the Philistines were still reveling in the arrogance of their power over him. Even Delilah was wallowing in the rewards of her deception. Then, they began to think of new ways to mock him even more.

Suddenly, one of the lords of the Philistines delivered what he thought was a brilliant idea. He thought they should offer a public sacrifice unto Dagon their god for delivering their enemy into their hands. And they wanted to offer this sacrifice to Dagon in his temple.

After hearing this idea, all of the Philistines' lords agree that it was a clever idea to make a public sacrifice to the god of their deliverance. Therefore, they set a date for this sacrificial gatherings so that thousands of their people could attend. However, God wanted to use this idea to bring their defeat into fruition.

And when the date had arrived to make the sacrifice, all of the lords of the Philistines gathered together in the temple of Dagon to offer this great sacrifice unto him. They had also invited thousands of their people to join with them in this ceremony to Dagon their god.

Indeed, the temple of this celebration was full of attendees, with thousands even on the roof. And it is believed that even Delilah were rejoicing among the jubilant crowd. Certainly, she wanted to be there in attendance so that she could revel in the excitement. For she was the queen of his deceptive capture.

Definitely, when this celebration began, they began to rejoice very loudly. In fact, the lords of the Philistines cried out in the ceremony, "Our god Dagon hath delivered Samson our enemy into our hand. He is the most powerful god."

And when the people heard the lords of the Philistines cry out, they gave great praises to their god Dagon as well. They also cried out, "Our god Dagon hath delivered into our hands our enemy, and the destroyer of our country, which slew many of us."

Undoubtedly, as their heart became more jolly and cheerful, the lords of the Philistines decided to make a toast to their god in mocking Samson. And they said, "Call for Samson, that he may entertain us while we toast to our god Dagon." Although they wanted Samson to perform before them, his God had made him to be the trigger to set the trap for their defeat.

Quickly, they called for Samson out of the prison house. And when he arrived, they yelled out to him to perform a fantastic feat with his strength. Regrettably, these triumphant Philistine lords had not paid attention that his hair had grown back. And they were completely unaware that his Nazarite vow had been renewed.

In fact, this jubilant crowd had started to have fun with Samson at his expense. They were shouting at him and mocking him. Even though he could not see, they wanted him to entertain them with a show of his great strength. And he started to perform before them to their liking. Meanwhile, the trap had been set.

Definitely, the lords of the Philistines and all of the people were enjoying the sporting atmosphere. They were also drinking plentiful amounts of alcohol and enjoy themselves in a merry way. They now had the strongman Samson to entertain them.

Now, Dagon's temple where this ceremony took place was a huge house. Its roof could hold up to three thousand spectators. And the temple could hold twice as many people on the inside. And this huge temple stood on two great pillars way above the ground.

Then, the lords of the Philistines had Samson placed between the two big pillars that held up the building. In this location, he was positioned where he could be seen by thousands of the excited spectators. The Philistine leaders wanted the people to see Samson's humiliation. But this location is where God wanted his servant Samson to be.

Samson's Final Revenge

CHAPTER 33

# Samson's Final Revenge in Dagon's Temple

At this time, the lords of the Philistines had planned to see Samson performed his great strength before this large gathering in an entertaining way. But contrariwise, God had planned to use Samson great strength in a more powerful way.

Certainly, He had decided to put an end to all of this idol worshipping of this false god Dagon and the mocking of His servant Samson. Therefore, He had intended to use Samson in a most explosive way. He wanted to get rid of all of the lords of the Philistines and those who had come to worship him. So, He put a thought in Samson's head.

Indeed, as Samson stood between the two big pillars that held up the building, he realized that two great pillars supported the whole house. Therefore, he said unto the young boy that held him by the hand, "Suffer me that I may feel the pillars whereupon the house standeth, that I may lean upon them." And when he did, the trigger was set and all of those who had attended were caught in the trap.

Now, for this ceremony, the house was full of men and women. In fact, all the lords of the Philistines were there. It is believed that Delilah was also among those who were with the lords of the Philistines. And upon the roof, there were about three thousand men and women that beheld while Samson entertain them.

Therefore, after Samson had touched the two big pillars, he knew that his vow to the Lord had been renewed. Then, he began to call unto the LORD. In fact, he cried out, "Dear God, you called me into this ministry before I was born. I ask you to restore my strength one more time. I want to show the Philistine that you are still God. And I want to avenge them for my two eyes."

Immediately, Samson took hold of the two middle pillars upon which the house stood, and which gave it all of it support. With a pillar in his right hand and a pillar in his left hand, he cried, "Let me die with the Philistines."

Then, he bowed himself with all his might; and the house fell and it was a great collapse. In fact, the building collapsed upon all of the lords of the Philistines, and upon all the people that were in the house including Delilah. So, the dead which he slew at his death were more than they which he slew in his life.

In Scripture, he said, "O Lord God, remember me, I pray thee, and strengthen me, I pray thee, only this once, O God, that I may be at once avenged of the Philistines for my two eyes. And Samson took hold of the two middle pillars upon which the house stood, and on which it was borne up, of the one with his right hand, and of the other with his left. And Samson said, Let me die with the Philistines. And he bowed himself with all his might; and the house fell upon the lords, and upon all the people that were therein. So the dead which he slew at his death were more than they which he slew in his life" (Judges 16:28-30).

Indeed, Samson also asked to die in this building collapse. And his prayer was honored. And with this massive destruction, God had completed His divine mission for Samson. He had avenged himself with the deaths of all of the leaders of the Philistines and the co-conspirator Delilah.

However, when his brethren and all the house of his father had heard of this tremendous collapse of this huge building, and the death of their brother Samson, they came down to Gaza. They discovered his body among the rubbish and took it up and brought it back home.

Then, they buried Samson in the same burying place of Manoah his father between Zorah and Eshtaol. And in the destruction of this huge temple and the killing of the Philistines, Samson had gotten his revenge in pulling down the two pillars for his two eyes.

Lastly, Samson was named among the people of faith, for he did it all unto the Lord his God. Truly, the Scripture said, "And what shall I more say? for the time would fail me to tell of Gedeon, and of Barak, and of Samson, and of Jephthae; of David also, and Samuel, and of the prophets: Who through faith subdued kingdoms, wrought righteousness, obtained promises, stopped the mouths of lions. Quenched the violence of fire, escaped the edge of the sword, out of weakness were made strong, waxed valiant in fight, turned to flight the armies of the aliens" (Hebrews 11:32-34).

Samson became the most famous of the judges of Israel, for he had obeyed his calling of God. He had been called of God to deliver Israel from the oppression and domination of the Philistines. And he was mightily used of God through his superhuman strength.

Without doubt, God is still calling all people to go and work for Him. And He promised to be with them throughout their calling. Therefore, today's Spirit-filled Believer should be actively defeating the domination and oppression of the devil in his or her daily life through the supernatural power of the Holy Spirit. With grace to all, and to God be the glory!

# Conclusion

From a biblical perspective, this inspiring narrative "**Israel's Intrepid Warrior: The Dauntless Courage of Samson**" magnificently portrayed Israel's deliverance from the domination of the Philistines. Through dramatic victories and devastating defeats for the Philistines, Samson miraculously completed his significant calling.

Remarkably, after more than four hundred years, the children of Israel had not conquered all of the Indigenous groups in this land of Canaan. For God had allowed those Indigenous groups to remain in the land of Canaan. So, when the children of Israel turned away from worshiping Him, He used one or more of those Indigenous group to chastise his people.

But when God chastised his people and they cry out to him for deliverance, His incomparable compassion comes quickly to their deliverance. Unquestionably, this narrative showed how God brought miraculous deliverance to the people of Israel.

Definitely, after the children of Israel had been chastised by the Philistines for their sins for forty years, God gave supernatural strength to a man called Samson, and he single-handedly delivered them from the oppression of their enemies.

Without doubt, Samson was indeed a miracle child. And he was born Nazarite from birth. He was raised in a traditional Jewish home. But with his supernatural strength, he became the one and only real life superman for Israel.

Ultimately, Samson became a man of superhuman physical strength against the Philistines and he slew thousands of them. And the Philistine rulers would do anything to learn where his great strength lies, for they wanted him dead.

Finally, Samson traveled to the valley of Sorek and met a Philistine maiden named Delilah. And when the lords of the Philistine learned of their affair, they conspired with each other to offered her a sum of money to work together with them to find the secret of Samson's great strength. She immediately agreed. And his deep love for her was his downfall.

Indeed, she enticed Samson repeatedly to tell her the secret of his strength. With her seduction and deception, she eventually weakened his desire to withhold his secret any longer. Then, he told her the secret of his great strength.

Then, she rushed and told the lords of the Philistines, and they quickly captured him. However, instead of killing him, the Philistines decided to humiliate him. They gouged out his eyes and put him in prison in Gaza to grind at the mill.

But God was not finished with Samson in his defeat of the Philistines. So, one day, the rulers of the Philistine decided to make a religious sacrifice to their god Dagon for having delivered Samson into their hands.

In fact, they assemble in the temple of Dagon to conduct this ritual. And while the temple of Dagon was crowded with thousands of the Philistine people who had come to mock Samson, they called for Samson so that people could watch him perform for them.

However, as Samson was being led into the temple, he asked his guide to lead him to the two pillars of the temple to rest. Then, he turned to the Lord and prayed. And God heard his prayer and restored his strength. He also asked to die with the Philistines.

Quickly, Samson took hold of the two pillars and pushed with all his might until the temple fell with a thunderous crash. This tremendous crash killed everyone else in the temple including Samson. So, in his death, he had killed more of his enemies than he had in all his life.

And when his brethren and all the house of his father had heard of his death, they came and retrieved his body. Then, they buried him near the tomb of his father Manoah. And, needless to say, Samson became the most famous of the judges of Israel, for he had delivered Israel from the oppression and domination of the Philistines through his superhuman strength. He had obeyed his calling of God.

Now, I turn to you, the reader. Our God is still calling men and women to work for Him in the mission of winning souls. Through the supernatural power of the Holy Spirit, God has also enabled Believers to be victorious.

Therefore, this author strongly believe that Spirit-filled Believers should be actively defeating the domination and oppression of the devil in their daily lives. For God promised to be with us throughout our calling. Therefore, with love, let's be about our Father's business. Withith grace and love to all, and to God be the glory!

# BIBLIOGRAPHY

Scofield, C.I. *The Scofield Study Bible.* Oxford University Press, New York, 2003, Print. The
  Holy Bible Authorized King James Version.

# SUGGESTED READINGS

Duffield, Guy P. and Van Cleave, Nathaniel M. *Foundations Of Pentecostal Theology*, Foursquare Media, Los Angeles, California, 1983.

Geisler, Norman L. *Systematic Theology*, Bethany House Publishing, Minneapolis, Minnesota, 2002.

Grudem, Wayne. *Systematic Theology: An Introduction To Biblical Doctrine*, Zondervan, Grand Rapid, Michigan, 1994.

Macdonald, William. *Believer's Bible Commentary.* Thomas Nelson Publishers, Nashville, Tennessee, 1989.

Menzies, William W. and Horton, Stanley M. Bible Doctrines: A Pentecostal Perspective, Gospel Publishing House, Springfield, Missouri, 1993.

Ryrie, Charles Caldwell. *Basic Theology: A Popular Systematic Guide to Understanding Biblical Truth*, Moody Publisher, Chicago, Illinois, 1986.

# INDEX

Ruse, 5, 64